KU-493-238

The **NO-NONSENSE GUIDE** to

FAIR TRADE

David Ransom

The No-Nonsense Guide to Fair Trade
First published in the UK by
New Internationalist™ Publications Ltd
Oxford OX4 1BW, UK
www.newint.org
New Internationalist is a registered trade mark.

First printed 2001. Revised edition 2002. Reprinted 2003, 2004. New
edition 2006. Reprinted 2009.

Cover image: Coffee beans/Corbis

© David Ransom/New Internationalist

All rights reserved. No part of this book may be reproduced, stored in a
retrieval system or transmitted, in any form or by any means, electronic,
electrostatic, magnetic tape, mechanical, photocopying, recording or
otherwise, without prior permission in writing of the Publisher.

Series editor: Troth Wells
Design by New Internationalist Publications Ltd.

 Printed on recycled paper by T J Press International, Cornwall, UK
who hold environmental accreditation ISO 14001.

British Library Cataloguing-in-Publication Data.
A catalogue record for this book is available from the British Library.

Library of Congress Cataloguing-in-Publication Data.
A catalogue for this book is available from the Library of Congress.

ISBN: 978-1904456-438

Foreword

'IS FAIR TRADE really fair?' This question, coming from a bright 10-year-old at a meeting between *adivasis* (indigenous peoples) from India and schoolchildren in Britain, took us completely by surprise. The children had been studying the story of the *adivasi* tea growers in a village called Chembakolli in the Gudalur valley, southern India. They are selling their tea directly to consumers through Just Change – a new initiative that seeks to take fair trade further.

ACCORD, the organization we work for in India, helped them to legalize possession of their ancestral lands by planting tea. While this raised their incomes, it also left them vulnerable to what are euphemistically called 'market forces'. Our search for a more secure market led us to the fair trade movement. It seemed like the answer to our prayers.

Fair trade was path-breaking. It moved the cheese. Shouting 'Fair Trade Not Aid!' changed the tune from charity to justice. Using the term 'fair' exposed the indigestible fact that world trade is unfair; that the rules are made to exploit poor countries and peoples.

The F word has become respectable. It's now on everyone's lips, out there in everyone's supermarket, so cool that even Nestlé – the world's biggest food corporation – has the gall to grab the brand and cash in on it.

So what's the next step? Can we allow obviously questionable organizations – like Nestlé – to usurp fair trade and the years of work done by its pioneers? Or can we move the goalposts and talk serious business for a change?

So far, fair trade has largely been the preserve of decent middle-class people who care about justice. Yet isn't it a sop to consumers' consciences, allowing them the feel-good factor? Buying fair trade is good for the soul, just as buying organic is good for the body.

But so far, from the producers' point of view it has meant little more than a move from greedy transnationals to apparently more benevolent ones. Minimum wages have come to be accepted as a basic right of workers the world over. A price the employer has to pay, no matter whether the business can afford it or not. But when it comes to small producers and farmers, why is a minimum price to cover the cost of production not seen as their fundamental right? All over the world we drive our small-scale farmers to death by exploiting them.

Though the hype appears to revolve around the producer getting a decent price, it is really about the consumer. Fair trade has to move on from being just another brand that allows consumers a choice. It has to change the power relationship between producers and the companies that buy their product – irrespective of whether these companies are rapacious transnationals or benevolent fair-trade ones.

Those British schoolkids knew their stuff and we had to think quite carefully before replying to their question. 'It's fair,' we conceded, 'but it could be fairer.' And that, in a nutshell, sums up the point we're at in the debate.

In this *No-Nonsense Guide to Fair Trade* David Ransom sets the context for this debate with first-hand stories from around the world. The debate will become more intense as the need for fundamental change to the unjust system of world trade grows more pressing. He points out that no-one is just a 'consumer' or a 'producer' – we are all both at the same time. He argues that the time has now come to put body and soul, justice and the environment, together. There's no time to lose.

Stan and Mari Marcel Thekaekara are founders of ACCORD, an organization that works with the tribal peoples of Gudalur, Tamil Nadu.

CONTENTS

Introduction

A whistle-stop tour through the history of international trade and a few snapshots of the scenery. How 'free' trade and the law of comparative advantage came to rule the roost, and who's been paying for the consequences. What fair trade is trying to do about it.

AS IN LOVE and war, all's fair in trade. The very idea of 'fair' trade looks, from one point of view, to be at once a statement of the obvious and a contradiction in terms. It's obvious that you can only buy something from someone who wants to sell, and vice versa – trade is a voluntary exchange between consenting adults and therefore fair by definition. Equally, 'fair' trade is a contradiction in terms because trading comes naturally to people and regulates itself through the self-righting mechanism of market forces. Morality simply doesn't come into it. You can't buck the market. As with rain forests or the ocean tides, you meddle with trade at your peril.

This orthodoxy has prevailed for a good while now and it might have a better claim to persist were it not so patently absurd. Who are these people who can't buck the market, a system they themselves invented, supposedly in their own best interests? What is the likeness between market and environmental forces, when the one conspires to destroy the other? Markets and trade are human constructs and therefore susceptible to human failings – not least in this respect, that by aspiring to infallibility they are less able to learn from their mistakes.

So what is fair in trade? Ask two simple questions: who benefits – and who is accountable? In the case of orthodox 'free' trade, the answer to the first question is straightforward: the already rich and powerful. It is, in other words, patently unfair. The answer to the second question is, if anything, even simpler: no-one. Unfair trade is the mortal enemy of democratic accountability, which gets in its way. Fair trade is primarily about reasserting human control over a mechanism that claims to be in the best interests of everyone but no longer even bothers to prove it.

History can tell us something about how we got into this fix. The word 'trade' has had a surprisingly short life in the English language but its meaning has changed even so. Originally it described a path or track marked out by the passage of human feet. From the 14th century onwards it was also applied to the course of a ship. By extension, it came to suggest a way of life as well. A couple of hundred years ago (and sometimes even now) people were said to 'follow a trade' – the craft of a stonemason, tailor or carpenter, who stood somewhere between 'professional' and 'laborer' in the hierarchy of class. To one side of grand entrances to stately homes and smart hotels you can still sometimes find signs indicating 'Tradesmen's Entrance' round the back. Only in the 20th century did trade come to signify exclusively the exchange of things for profit. The process by which a way of life became a way of making money tells us most of what we need to know about the trouble with the word as it's currently understood.

The adjective 'free' creates other difficulties when attached to it, as routinely happens in orthodox economics. In the 19th century, industrial capitalism spread around the world through the muscular sinews of European empires. Most of them had been founded on military conquest and were maintained by brute force. They operated a variety of 'mercantilist' trading systems which prohibited commercial exchange with rival empires – or anyone else – without official approval and profit. The ultimate purpose of foreign trade was to enrich and glorify the rulers of the colonial power, whether that was Spain, Portugal, France, Britain or Holland.

Introduction

Comparative advantage

As industrial capitalism grew in wealth and power, particularly in Britain, it was in need of a theory to justify why it, rather than assorted royalty and landed gentry, should be the legitimate heir to the riches that could be harvested from international trade. The theory of 'comparative advantage' was deployed early in the 19th century to explain why trade unencumbered by mercantilist restrictions would eventually be better for everyone – and, quite coincidentally of course, industrial capitalists too. Interminable, arcane disputes between free-traders and their rivals began and continue along remarkably similar lines to this day.

The notion of comparative advantage is usually attributed to the British millionaire stockbroker and entrepreneur David Ricardo. It was a refinement of the theory of 'absolute advantage' first devised by Adam Smith. According to this theory, every part of the world has an economic advantage of some sort. So, for example, Britain in the early 19th century had an advantage in the industrial manufacture of cloth. It had liberal supplies of coal, made the steam engines that powered the mills and, as people were forced off the land into industrial cities, plentiful labor to work them. The former British colony in America, on the other hand, had an abundance of agricultural land, a shortage of urban labor and, in the south, the right climate for growing cotton. So it made sense for America to send cotton for manufacture into cloth in Britain and to buy cotton cloth from Britain in return. Both countries were better off this way, making the most of their advantage and the 'international division of labor', than they would have been if they had each tried to do exactly the same thing.

'Comparative advantage' complicated matters somewhat by suggesting that advantages operated within as well as between national economies. So, for example, although England produced both wheat and iron more cheaply than Poland, its comparative advantage in iron was greater than its absolute advantage in wheat. So it made sense for England to import wheat from Poland, even though its own wheat was produced more efficiently. Poles would be better off because it cost them less labor to buy English iron with their wheat than to produce iron themselves. The English would be better off because it would pay the Poles to offer sufficient wheat for English iron to make them net gainers too. In this way, international trade worked to maximize the efficiency of every national economy. Hard to prove, but in the right voice it could be made to sound pretty convincing.

Ricardo or Marcet?

The trouble with this proposition begins at the very beginning, for it was not David Ricardo who first came up with it. Mrs Jane Marcet was a prolific author of textbooks on topics as diverse as chemistry and philosophy and wrote fictional 'conversations' between girl students and their teachers. A year before Ricardo published his *Principles of Political Economy, and Taxation*, Mrs Marcet's *Conversations on Political Economy* appeared with the more or less complete theory of comparative advantage set out in the form of a dialogue between 'Caroline' and 'Mrs B'. Needless to say, her contribution has gone largely unrecognized and the attribution to Ricardo remains. Economic orthodoxy is as susceptible to prevailing prejudice – in this case, the inferiority of women and the superiority of stockbrokers – as any other.

So, when it comes to comparing advantages, the view you take rather depends on where you stand. Aspiring US capitalists, for example, had good reason to appreciate the disadvantages of comparative advantage. More profit could be made from cotton cloth than from raw cotton. The process of industrial manufacture added 'value', which was reflected in the high price of the cloth relative to the raw cotton commodity. Americans could capture more of this value, in profits and employment, if the cotton mills were in America rather than Britain. Comparative advantage as it was interpreted in imperial Britain at the time would have kept American cotton producers comparatively poor while making British mill owners very much richer ad infinitum. American capitalists got upset about this sort of thing. It just wasn't fair. After all, they had put up much of the cash for the war of independence from Britain that would eventually launch the American capitalist juggernaut – and American cotton cloth, like denim – onto an unsuspecting world.

Slave labor

The cotton fields of the American south were, of course, run on slave labor. For hundreds of years the slave trade had operated much like any other, if a great deal more profitably than most. From the point of view of America's cotton barons, slavery must have looked like an advantage to beat all others – without it there would have been no cotton business at all. The freedom to indulge in it was as stoutly advocated then as free trade is today. However, those budding industrial capitalists couldn't operate their new factories on slave labor. Slavery worked very profitably in rural, agricultural settings, but not in industrial, urban ones, where a wage-earning workforce had to be hired and fired at will. Slavery undermined the 'free' market for labor – like any other commodity – that the industrial revolution required. That was one of the issues on which the American Civil War was fought and won – in good measure by the wealth of industrial capitalists once again.

The Great Depression

In other words, it is quite impossible to detach economic orthodoxy from the prevailing disposition of wealth, power and self-interest. The more you think about it, the more absurd becomes the notion that 'free' trade has ever existed – or ever will. The clearest indication of this comes from those regular occasions when capitalism goes into one of its slumps or depressions. The worst of these – so far – was the Great Depression of the 1930s, in the brief years between the two great wars, when the system itself seemed to be on the verge of collapse. Today's free-traders will tell you that what went wrong then was that governments tried to protect their national industries from the effects of depression by raising tariffs against foreign competitors, thereby stalling international trade and compounding the ruin. This interpretation has given 'protectionism' a bad name ever since.

Less partisan accounts, however, also notice parallels between the generally indolent stance of governments towards the internal workings of their national economies – and mass unemployment in particular – in the 1930s, and the inertia of national governments in the face of free-market 'globalization' today. Leastways, capitalism in America recovered in the 1940s only with the aid of lavish government spending on employment programs and the Second World War – scarcely a prime example of the self-righting mechanisms and benign effects of free-market forces. After the experience of the 1930s and 1940s, a conscious effort was made to industrialize the newly independent colonies of Europe in Africa and Asia, as well as Latin America, in the 1950s and 1960s. That way, it was felt, nation-building could begin and international markets for industrial goods would expand much faster, to the benefit of everyone. In the South, government programs of 'import substitution' encouraged 'infant industries' to set themselves up, protected behind tariff barriers against foreign competition.

In some places, like Japan and the Little Tigers of Southeast Asia – notably Hong Kong, Singapore,

Introduction

Taiwan and South Korea – this worked pretty well. With their own new industries protected behind import barriers, these countries set out to be 'export-oriented' and produce things for world markets. In other places – particularly in Africa and Latin America – it worked pretty badly, creating inefficient industries that limped along, trying to supply local markets and consuming enormous subsidies, until they finally expired. Nonetheless, international trade and the world economy experienced its 'golden age' of growth.

Export-led growth

By the 1970s the failures of import-substitution were too obvious to ignore. When combined with the collapse of the Soviet Union after 1989, they gave the free-marketeers renewed determination and confidence. Even if the free market proved as disastrous as before, what was the alternative? A fashion for 'export-led' economic growth began to sweep the world, based on the success of the Little Tigers. The idea was that, since world trade tends to grow faster than individual economies, producing for 'world markets' would be the most efficient and profitable way ahead. Deregulation removed the very idea that governments could usefully intervene. The results have been very satisfactory indeed for the chief advocates of the experiment – banks and transnational corporations. For almost everyone else, and particularly since the crisis in the Little Tigers that exploded in 1997, they have been very much less obvious.

Many of the countries of the South remain today just as they have always been, entirely dependent on producing basic commodities like cotton for world markets. Their experience of world trade has been utterly disastrous, and for reasons that are not in dispute. There is no quicker way to make – or lose – a fortune than by speculating on international

The origins of the World Trade Organization

As World War Two came to an end, a spirit of 'never again' prevailed over international affairs. This led to the founding of the United Nations in 1945. The original intention was to create subsidiary agencies accountable to the UN, including the financial institutions that eventually became the World Bank and International Monetary Fund. There were plans for an International Trading Organization.

Powerful interests succeeded in separating the economic from the political institutions. A General Agreement on Tariffs and Trade (GATT), with just 23 of the West's richest countries was founded in 1948. Its purpose was to resolve trade disputes through a series of negotiating 'rounds', the last of which was launched in Uruguay in 1987. One of the agreements eventually reached by the 'Uruguay Round' was that GATT should transform itself into the World Trade Organization (WTO). GATT had no legal means of enforcing its decisions. The advance of globalization opened up the prospect of a truly global agency enforcing free-market values with an armory of sanctions and fines. Meanwhile, the collapse of the Soviet Union and the end of the Cold War created a large number of potential new members.

The WTO was set up in 1995. Trade negotiations would be conducted in the single currency of the market – hard cash. 'Process' issues affecting the environment or human rights were excluded. Although most countries now belong to the WTO, many cannot even afford to be represented, while a few of the most powerful routinely make decisions on their own in what's become known as the 'Green Room'.

The first serious challenge to these values came at the Ministerial Meeting of the WTO in Seattle in 1999, where plans for a 'Millennium Round' of negotiations had to be put on hold. After this experience, the WTO moved its next Ministerial meeting to the relative isolation of Doha, Qatar in 2001. There, despite attempts to proclaim a new 'Development Round', the agenda continued to reflect the interests of powerful countries and corporations.

These interests congealed into an attempt to broaden the agenda to even more contentious political territory, such as investment, public services or government procurement, at the Ministerial Meeting in Cancún, Mexico, in 2003. Here, for the first time, a 'Group of 20' developing countries (including some large ones such as Brazil and India) began to discuss their position separately, though to little tangible effect in the run-up to the next Ministerial Meeting in Hong Kong in 2005, where inertia ruled again.

The US and European Union have focused on direct 'bilateral' trade agreements with Southern governments in an attempt to nullify any concerted effort by the Group of 20 and others at the WTO. A stalemate has been reached, allowing the inequities and hypocrisies of the current system to continue more or less unchecked. ∎

commodity markets. A frost kills the coffee harvest in Brazil; a war disrupts copper supplies from Zambia; a speculator attempts to 'corner' the silver market: all such events cause sharp fluctuations in prices and unequaled opportunities for profit – or loss. The effect is compounded by vast amounts of money switching in and out of commodity markets in London, New York or Chicago. Even larger sums of speculative money swill around the currencies in which world trade is transacted. So the soundest financial advice is always to avoid commodity markets like the plague – unless you can afford to lose your money. Today, the poorest countries least able to afford it are the most heavily reliant on world commodity markets for their very survival. This is about as close to economic insanity as it is possible to get, though economic orthodoxy insists that they must get closer still.

Deep in debt

In good measure because of this, many such countries are now deeply in debt. So they have been forced by their rich creditors into 'structural adjustment' – subsequently restyled 'poverty reduction' or 'poverty alleviation' – programs. These are a form of bankruptcy administration, modified only by the fact that you can't liquidate a country or a people in quite the same way as you can a company or a corporation. Among other things, the programs require debtors to export whatever commodities they can lay their hands on in order to earn foreign currency with which to service their debts. Because every debtor is ordered to do this at the same time, there follows an entirely predictable glut of commodities on world markets – and prices plummet.

The winners once again are speculators, banks and corporations, as well as everyone in the North who benefits from the low levels of inflation that cheap commodities from the South make possible. The losers are the world's environment – as precious nonrenewable resources are wrenched out and recklessly squandered – and poor people's redoubled impoverishment. So the free-trade balance looks very much less favorable when viewed from the South, from where the majority of the world's people see it. Some advantages on world markets are evidently more comparative than others.

International trade now, at the outset of the 21st century, looks very different from the way it did at the outset of the 20th century. The European empires have almost vanished. In their place is a single empire of footloose corporate capital, dominated by the United States.

Associated with this is a profound change: the majority of the world's manufacturing labor force has moved from the North to the cheap-labor countries of the South. In export-processing zones that run in a band around the most heavily populated regions of the world, from Mexico and Central America through the Philippines, Indonesia and China to India, Pakistan and Morocco, many millions of people live and work in conditions resembling most closely those of 19th-century Europe or America. In China in particular a toxic mix of economic neo-liberalism with political authoritarianism and a huge concentration of foreign investment has produced dramatic results in enclaves of modernity. A similar pattern has begun to develop in India. However, doubts about long-term sustainability – whether economic or environmental – persist.

As the hard labor of manufacturing has moved South, so 'post-industrial', 'post-modern' or 'information' economies seem to have emerged in the North. In reality, things still have to be made, but power and wealth have slipped away from industrial labor into the hands of the corporate citadels and finance houses of the North. For the majority of the world's population in the South, the advent of the new century has

The terms of trade

A key element of international trade is the 'terms' on which it takes place. Individual countries earn foreign currency from exports and spend it on imports. So, for example, one country might export rice and import oil. If the world price of rice halves, or the price of oil doubles, then it will have to export twice as much rice to import the same amount of oil. Its 'terms of trade' are then said to have worsened or become more 'adverse'.

The critical thing is not just the price of rice, but its price relative to everything else. This is the problem with exporting commodities such as coffee beans, or raw materials. It's not just that the 'added value' of processing the coffee beans is lost to the exporting country. Over the years, the world price of commodities has tended to fall relative to everything else. So any country that exports the former and imports the latter is in trouble.

This is what still happens in the poorest countries in the world, particularly in Africa. A hungry country might find itself exporting more and more food grains because that's all it has, despite the fact that the world price has fallen. Food gets scarcer at home and its price might actually increase for the local population. Very often, imports considered 'essential' by local élites are of things like cars which benefit only them. In this way, worsening terms of trade are felt in declining standards of living and increased poverty.

But it's not just 'physical' trade that matters. Commodity exports are used to pay rich countries for foreign debts – so even more has to be exported, and world prices fall still further, without increasing the wealth of poor countries at all. It's a downward spiral with no obvious end.

Taking from the poor to give to the rich is the only guiding principle. ■

The terms of trade in Africa

This chart shows how a sharp decline in Africa's terms of trade between 1997 and 1998 was matched by a severe fall in real incomes.

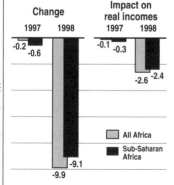

Human Development Report 1999, UNDP.

been accompanied by a retreat into the conditions of an increasingly distant past.

Where the power lies

Then, as now, the most pressing issue for everyone caught up in the maelstrom was the absence of any notion that people should, or could, intervene in their shared destiny. Most of our democratic aspirations today are focused on national or local governments – but most of the decisions that matter are taken by transnational corporate empires, backed by the United States.

These empires are the most active advocates of 'free' world trade simply because they monopolize two-thirds of it – a much greater share than they have of internal or 'domestic' trade – and want to keep it that way. They do not mean 'free' in the common sense of the word; merely that it should continue to operate in their interests.

Paradoxically, they rely very heavily indeed on governments to achieve this. They receive lavish cash handouts from the public purse: subsidies, bailouts (for banks in particular), tax breaks, 'incentives', hard currencies in which to do business, 'diplomatic' assistance and commercial espionage, publicly funded scientific research, government contracts, credit guarantees, 'policing' operations like the World Trade Organization (WTO), an educated, trained and compliant workforce, roads, ports, airports – more or less anything that takes their fancy.

Such is the extent of public subsidy to private, corporate enterprise that it is they, rather than those who rely on meager welfare benefits, who truly deserve the title 'scroungers'. In return they fund political parties in rich countries, sponsor corrupt individuals in poor ones – which comes much cheaper, but amounts to the same thing – and gain a political stranglehold as well.

Introduction

Controlling the beast
The question is not whether intervention in trade is necessary or desirable, but what kind of intervention there is to be; not whether trade should be 'regulated' or 'deregulated', but whether it is to be the servant or the master of people. Though the human interest in this matter may have only the faintest of voices at present, it is getting very much louder because the most urgent priorities for the majority of the world's people are so similar.

The first is inequality. A cornucopia of things may have been conjured into existence, but it is available only to a small and shrinking proportion of the world's people – at best, just 20 per cent. Because the wealth of unrestrained capitalism doesn't just exist, but accumulates, left to its own devices it makes the rich relatively richer, the poor relatively poorer and the gap between the two absolutely wider at an accelerating, compound rate. Democracy cannot conceivably survive, let alone flourish, within or between societies where such blatant injustice intensifies by the day.

The second concerns the nature of capitalist wealth itself. For example, everyone knows that climate change is already upon us and has to be halted – or there will be an end to our children's children. Yet prevailing economic orthodoxy dictates that there is nothing much to be done about it.

The birth of fair trade
Just as well, then, that for the past 30 years or so a small but determined and growing band of pioneers has been working on the practicalities of trade done rather differently. Can it be made to work for, rather than against, commodity producers in the South? Can the process of production be democratized, ownership shared, organized labor encouraged, child labor made unnecessary, environmental sustainability and human rights promoted? Can consumers be induced to think

Consuming passions

There's a scale of inequity that varies with different kinds of consumption. Basic necessities like food grains are consumed in a broadly equal fashion by the world's population. High-protein foodstuffs like fish or meat are less evenly distributed between rich and poor. Consumption of electricity, telephones and paper is progressively more concentrated in the hands of the rich. At the extreme, 90 per cent of all private motor cars are owned by the richest 20 per cent of the world's population. Four-fifths of total consumption expenditure is accounted for by just one-fifth of the world's population.

Measured in terms of environmental costs, rather than just money, the inequity is even more extreme because the rich consume much more of the things that cost the environment most, like fossil fuels and metals. We shall, of course, have exterminated ourselves entirely before the rates of car ownership in, say, the US are ever replicated across the world's population as a whole. That means dealing with the private motor car in the North, rather than turning for salvation to the further impoverishment of the South.

Conventional notions of 'wealth' tend to create an autocracy of consumption. The contrast between rich and poor gets sharper the more 'advanced' the technology involved – the majority of the world's population has yet to speak on the telephone, for example.

As a general principle, the closer wealth is to being equitably shared, the more 'sustainable' it is likely to be. Fair trade is also about the role world trade plays, for good or ill, in this process. ∎

Shares of world consumption*

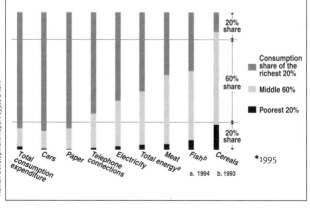

*1995

a. 1994 b. 1993

Human Development Report 1998, UNDP.

– and pay – more than they currently appear to believe is necessary? Is it possible to survive, even to prosper, both 'in' and 'against' the conventional marketplace? Is there any 'bottom line' other than price and profit?

The idea of fair trade is not new. In its contemporary form it has developed in parallel with the process of globalization. From the 1970s onwards, aid agencies and their associates have been working with craftspeople in the South to satisfy a taste for 'ethnic' household goods and ornaments in the North. Solidarity movements with places like Nicaragua began to make use of trade in traditional Southern commodities, such as coffee, to increase awareness and raise funds. More recently, fair trade has moved on to use conventional retail and marketing methods across a range of tropical food products, looking for a wider impact on the 'mainstream' through supermarkets and sophisticated advertising campaigns.

One way or another, unfair free trade is now on trial. That involves discovering exactly how and by whom the things we consume are made, and examining the evidence. Conventional trade relies on our remaining blind to this kind of evidence. The greatest single virtue of fair trade is that it encourages us to take a closer look, to engage more critically with the intriguing, sometimes shameful, details of everyday life. This *No-Nonsense Guide* considers fair trade in its wider sense, as the seed of an alternative that can flourish more vigorously than is sometimes assumed. Little attention has yet been paid to the subject – there are, for example, precious few books on fair trade. Meanwhile, there is something practical that more or less any of us can do to promote fair trade in our daily lives, by searching out and supporting those alternatives that are already available.

It's tempting to dismiss the topic as impenetrably tedious. After all, people must adapt to overpowering realities, learn to compete on world markets or simply go under – so what's the point of quibbling? Common sense, however, suggests a degree of caution when we're presented too bluntly with a reality to which there is said to be no alternative. Almost certainly, someone is trying to conceal the options that do exist. In this case at least one alternative is to follow more closely the path trade takes and to listen to the untidy human story that is told in the chapters that follow.

We begin by looking at one country, Mexico, at a critical time in its recent history, when it was on the verge of signing the North American Free Trade Agreement (NAFTA). Mexico is the only Southern country that borders directly on the US, so the issues here are in very sharp focus. We pay a brief visit to coffee producers in the southern state of Chiapas just before New Year's Day 1994 – a critical date here, since as well as the signing of NAFTA it marked the start of an uprising that still makes waves around the world.

In the second chapter we meet the *cafeteleros* – coffee farmers – of south-eastern Peru, at the start of the long and winding road the coffee bean follows to reach its international market. Along the way we encounter a recurrent theme – the impact of international trade on local environments, in this case on the valley of the great Tambopata River at the headwaters of the Amazon.

The cocoa trail

For the third chapter we go to Ghana, a country that relies on the export of cocoa beans for all sorts of basic necessities, including government revenues. Ghana is in the grip of a 'poverty reduction' program imposed by the International Monetary Fund (IMF) and World Bank. As it turns out, the results for the cocoa farmers, who were supposed to be among the winners, have been ambiguous to say the least, though fair-trade co-operation makes a difference.

Bananas have lent their name to a variety of repub-

Introduction

lics and wars. Chapter Four reports from the battle-field of a recent Banana War in Central America and the Caribbean. From the plantations of Guatemala and the small farms of Dominica (one of the Windward Islands) there are some unexpected lessons for the High Court of Globalization, otherwise known as the WTO. Not least of these is the way it has, in effect, been promoting slave labor and environmental insanity. Lost in the fog of war, you wouldn't really expect to discover a perfect, fairly traded, organic banana – unless, that is, you chanced upon it in the Dominican Republic.

With the shift of manufacturing labor from North to South there's plenty of territory for fair trade to invade beyond traditional commodities. Blue jeans

The measure of fairness

It would be easy for fair-traders in the North to get carried away by the need to agree and enforce common standards. However, they have to take great care. Unless Southern producers are involved in the process from the start, then fair trade simply replicates the consumers' control over producers.

There are two main 'umbrella' groups to which most fair-trade organizations around the world now belong. Fair Trade Labeling Organizations International (FLO) is based in Bonn, Germany, and brings together a growing number of fair-trade labels. For some time it has been developing closer links with producers. The International Federation for Alternative Trade (IFAT), which recently moved its headquarters to the Netherlands, is a global network of 160 fair-trade organizations, many of them producers, in more than 50 countries. It is controlled by its membership.

FLO and IFAT have different functions and therefore slightly different standards – not all of their members necessarily observe them all, and neither FLO nor IFAT has direct power over its membership, though peer-group pressure is strong.

These are some common principles of fair trade:
• **Democratic organization** – producers must be able to exercise control, by owning the land on which they work, by being organized into co-operative or democratic associations or in other ways appropriate to particular settings.
• **Recognized trade unions** – where ownership is vested in others, then

are something of an icon for consumer capitalism, but the consequences of the trade that makes them are pernicious and reach round the world. Chapter Five suggests that consumer capitalism, replete as it is with fashionable brands, can't actually deliver on the promise it makes of unlimited choice, even between pairs of blue jeans.

In Chapter Six, we catch up with the cocoa beans from Ghana again as they find their way around corporate Big Chocolate in Britain. Under the watchful eye of Koto Asamoah Serebour, some of them also get into fair trade – and a much better deal for farmers like him. For the time being, far too much still depends on the strange and manipulated tastes of the consumer, but here at least there are some excellent alternatives on offer.

workers producing for fair trade must have the right to organize and negotiate through free trade unions.

• **No child labor** – though this is a much more complex issue than is sometimes suggested, its use is incompatible with fair trade.

• **Decent working conditions** – the above measures help to create good working conditions and pay, but there is a need to ensure them independently as well.

• **Environmental sustainability** – fair trade is becoming increasingly 'green', in part because prices for greener products (like organic food) are generally higher, but primarily because producers themselves prefer it.

• **Price that covers the cost of production** – this usually means providing a minimum-price guarantee, regardless of world commodity prices.

• **Social premiums to improve conditions** – in many cases a premium is paid that doesn't go directly to individual producers but to their organizations or communities for collective projects.

• **Long-term relationships** – which extend beyond specific contracts to purchase and may involve a much longer-term commitment if mutually-agreed conditions are met. This matters both to producers (so that they can have some certainty for the future) and to fair-trade purchasers, so that supplies are available even in the rare 'boom' years when prices are high and the need for fair trade seems less pressing. ∎

Introduction

Fair trade – the way forward

The episodes of this story have been gathered together from accounts first published in the New Internationalist magazine over the past decade or so. The ones about cocoa are the work of my colleague in Toronto, Richard Swift. The rest are mine, though subsequent events have made some updating necessary. For the most part, much less has changed than would have been both possible and desirable.

This remains the case despite the second revision of the text since its original publication in 2001. Tables and statistics have been updated and modified where appropriate, though the temptations of hindsight have been resisted. There is a completely revised final chapter, reflecting the real progress that fair trade has made in recent years, as well as the new dilemmas this has thrown up. Not least among these is the granting of 'Fairtrade' certification to products from transnational corporations like Nestlé and Kraft – a difficult issue that is discussed in some detail. Meanwhile, the orthodoxy of foul trade, epitomized by the WTO, lumbers on largely unreconstructed.

In any event, the point still is to restore to trade its essential purpose – either it enhances human well-being in general or it is a worthless enterprise that enriches some, impoverishes many more and gets us all precisely nowhere. The commitments made to each other by fair-traders invariably offend in some way against the law of comparative advantage and so are potentially subversive. For current economic orthodoxy to prevail, and for the horizons of what is conceivable to remain so meanly restricted, all that is required is for the alternatives to be made to seem irrelevant. The stories that follow show just what nonsense that really is.

1 Mexico: a cautionary tale

How international trade affects a whole country. What the North American Free Trade Agreement (NAFTA) was supposed to do for the only Southern country that borders on the United States – and what actually happened. How coffee farmers in Chiapas can tell the difference between 'free' and fair trade.

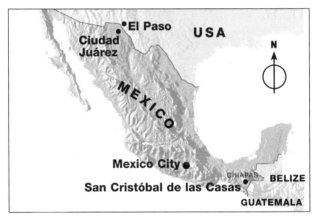

THE AVERAGE MEXICAN is neither desperately poor nor disgustingly rich. That, at any rate, is what the conventional economic measure of 'Gross National Product per capita' in Mexico tells you – what the place looks like if you average out its wealth across the population as a whole. The trouble is that wealth in Mexico is not averaged out equally across the population. In 2002 Mexico had the fourth-largest number of dollar billionaires in the world – the 35 richest families controlled as much wealth between them as its 15 million poorest citizens. That, rather than the average, is what makes Mexico characteristic of the world as a whole.

Unfair international trade transfers wealth from relatively poor countries to relatively rich ones. But it also transfers wealth between rich and poor people within individual countries. Governments of all kinds – local, regional or national; democratic or otherwise – are told that they cannot act to restore some measure of equity or environmental sanity to the process without contravening the laws of free trade, placing themselves beyond the pale of market forces and even the 'international community' itself.

Preparing for NAFTA

In September of 1993 I went to Mexico to research a magazine about the country. The Governments of Mexico, the US and Canada were putting the final touches to the North American Free Trade Agreement (NAFTA). It was due to come into effect on 1 January 1994, bringing down most of the remaining trade barriers between the three countries, ostensibly to the benefit of all concerned. With its huge pool of cheap labor, Mexico's enviable comparative advantage in labor costs would surely now be able to take full effect, and some very rich Mexicans expected to get very much richer as a result.

The official mood in the country was euphoric. The Mexican Government had outspent every other lobby-ist in Washington to help see NAFTA through the US Congress, and had begun to believe its own publicity. Mexico was about to defy the geographical imperative, kick the dust of its desert frontier with the US from its shoes and join the North. At the Mexico City head-quarters of the PRI (the Institutional Revolutionary Party), which had ruled the country since 1929, spokeswoman Roberta Lajous explained to me just how ambitious their plans were. 'If I could move the whole of Mexico to Europe I would,' she said. 'In fact, it would fit rather neatly into the Mediterranean Sea.' The aphorism that Mexico is eternally 'so far from God, so close to the United States' would lose its relevance. As it turned out, the PRI was also about to lose its grip on political power. Skeptics there were, to be sure. The economist Ifigenia Martínez of the Party of Democratic Revolution (PRD) told me: 'It will prove impossible to continue with this rotten system. It is constructed to serve the interests of very, very few people, and it simply cannot continue.' It was hard to square the PRI gloss with what I had already seen in Ciudad Juárez. This is the Mexican half of a sprawling desert city that straddles the border with the US and becomes El Paso, Texas, on the other side of the Rio Grande. Ciudad Juárez has mushroomed around its export-processing *maquiladoras* – the cheap-labor, export-only assembly sheds run by big-brand corporations that were the focus of all those official hopes for a bright future in Mexico City. I managed, with some difficulty and the help of a local collective of prostitutes, to get into a *maquila* making television sets for the giant Dutch electronics corporation, Philips.

Inside a *maquila*

'You enter a spotless cavern housing two writhing conveyor belts,' I wrote at the time, 'queen insects tended by straight lines of rigid young women in colored bibs, perhaps a hundred seated down either side of each monstrous beast, fed with components at one end and churning out cardboard boxes like square eggs filled with TVs at the other... This is work that almost anyone can do and no-one with any real choice in the matter really wants... No-one lingers here. There is no human contact, no conversation. A canteen serving food during the break is deserted – two died recently of poisoning after eating in a maquila canteen down the road. We manage to talk to some of the women before their shift starts: mere children, they seem, in their bibs. Some of them are. Others are on the verge of tears. "I sleep and I work. I can do nothing else," one of them says. For this they are paid $30 a week and are not allowed to complain... Their young lives are scarred: materially, emotionally, physically and permanently. This is crude and scandalous exploitation. No amount of globaloney can obscure it.'

Resistance grows

Much the same impression was inescapable if you talked to any of the myriad citizens' groups or trade unions in Mexico City – then the largest city in the world, and one of the most polluted. The Zócalo, the immense central square, was filled with wood smoke from the encampments of squatters from all over the country seeking to petition the President, whose official palace formed one side of the square – a metaphor for the condition of formal politics in Mexico at the time, since the President was rarely there.

The impression that all was not exactly as the advocates of NAFTA would have it grew stronger the further south I traveled. I eventually reached Chiapas, dubbed by people in Mexico City as the 'crazy' state – the majority indigenous population make it more akin to neighboring Guatemala than to the rest of Mexico. On 15 September, Independence Day, I watched the celebrations in the old colonial capital, San Cristóbal de las Casas, high in the Chiapas mountains. The entertainers for the public show were all imported by the local political élite from elsewhere in the country. On the hillsides around the city, wood fires twinkled like stars pinpointing where communities of indigenous people looked down – or perhaps turned their backs – on the festivities in the valley below.

Just a third of the Mexican population, some 30 million people, still made their living from the land. But that was more than had lived in the entire country just 50 years earlier. Mexico could not feed itself. The answer, according to the Harvard Business School graduates in Mexico City, lay with comparative advantage: sell tropical fruit to the Americans and buy cheap maize back. At the price of subsidized, imported US maize, however, none of the eight million small farmers in Mexico whose lives and cultures depended upon cultivating it could possibly survive. They would have to move to the cities and offer themselves up for work in the maquilas, just as required.

'Here the "modern" way of industrial agriculture is not appropriate,' José Juarez Varela told me, in his office in Las Margaritas, near the Guatemalan border. He worked for the *Union de Ejidos de la Selva* (the Union of Rural Collectives in the Forest). 'We have no infrastructure, roads, communications, technical services, and the urban markets are a long way away. The land is extremely delicate and mountainous, unsuitable for machinery. Even agricultural reform [following the revolution that began in 1910] arrived here late. It wasn't until the 1950s that people started leaving the *fincas*, the great private estates, freeing themselves from debt-bondage and setting up *ejidos*, collective farms. They began to move into the forest and to grow whatever they were used to growing; bananas, maize, coffee.'

New markets

The *ejidos* joined together to form a Union. 'We learned a lot and we had a good time,' said José, 'but we weren't making a living.' The Union went through a crisis. Some felt like giving up. José and a small group toured the country in search of fresh ideas. In Oaxaca, the neighboring state to the north, they met up with a group of farmers who were producing coffee for the Max Havelaar fair-trade label in the Netherlands.

On their return they decided to develop coffee production for niche export markets, including Max Havelaar. This meant a very different relationship with coffee buyers, cutting out the *coyote* middlemen and obtaining a guaranteed minimum price in exchange for guaranteed quality. The Union bought an old cotton warehouse and converted it into a coffee storage and grading plant. Most of its production still went onto

Cheap labor and the *maquiladoras*

From the mid-1960s onwards in Mexico – as in many other Central American countries – a new craze began for 'export-processing' assembly factories. Designated areas could operate outside the normal mass of regulations, importing raw materials or parts and exporting the product to the US. The proliferation of such factories around the world was one of the motive forces behind globalization. Most of the factories are either directly owned by transnational corporations or contracted to supply them. Much of the trade is between different parts of the same corporation.

Employment in such plants in Mexico, originally located for convenience on the border with the US, increased rapidly to nearly half a million by 1992 and nearer three million shortly thereafter. Over the years the maquilas have spread away from the US border and begun to recruit from Mexico's large indigenous population in the central highlands. The biggest single sector is transport (mostly automobiles), followed by electronics and textiles.

The main reason for establishing these factories was, of course, the cheap labor they could employ. Crude assembly work requires manual dexterity and minimal education – young women were considered particularly well-suited to this kind of work, provided they didn't get pregnant. Organized labor was invariably banned. Many workers in the US complained about the impact on their own wage levels and employment of these 'runaway' jobs.

The justification for them was that they increased employment for millions of Mexicans who were desperately in need of it. If working conditions were often very bad, they would improve with time.

In fact, wage levels in the maquilas – as in Mexico as a whole – fell relentlessly as the numbers employed in them rose, particularly following economic crises like the one in 1982, which was to prove the model for subsequent 'structural adjustment' policies around the world. ■

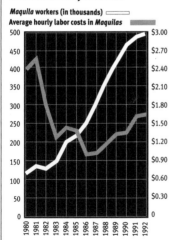

Hourly cost of labor and growth of employment in the early years of Mexican *maquiladoras*

Maquila workers (in thousands) ▭
Average hourly labor costs in *Maquilas* ▬

Harry Browne and Beth Sims, *Runaway America*, Resource Center Press, Alburquerque, New Mexico, 1993.

the ordinary commercial market, but after the collapse of world coffee prices in 1989 fair trade kept the Union alive. When I visited, it had just begun production for Twin Trading and Cafédirect in Britain, and for some specialist coffee traders in the US.

Down on the coffee farm

The following day we drove for three hours along broken roads to Cruz del Rosario, the nearest coffee-producing *ejido*. We had to announce our arrival at some distance from the village by sounding the truck horn three times – a reminder of growing tension and that intruders here were not always well-intentioned. We were greeted by a group of *ejidatarios* and eventually descended to the tropical forest in the valley below, where coffee bushes grew under the shade of forest trees. The ground was precipitous and had to be terraced. Rocks and boulders had to be shifted by hand. The farmers were moving to organic production which meant that no pesticides could be used to fend off disease – and no chemical fertilizers either. Compost was laboriously prepared from animal droppings and leaf-mould.

I wondered whether all this additional labor, even for a better price, really paid off. 'We are doing it for future generations,' replied Cirilo, who was taking me round.

This was the first time I had encountered fair trade on the ground in the South. I said to them that I would write about their work and perhaps, just perhaps, a few more people would buy their coffee in the North – not all of us were of one mind with the corporate agenda. I had no doubt at all that what Max Havelaar and Twin Trading were doing there was important. The Union felt it had a real status of partnership. Without fair trade, small as it was, these people's lives would have been very much more difficult.

On 1 January 1994, deliberately timed to coincide

NAFTA, FTAA amd all that

A North American Free Trade Agreement (NAFTA) between the US, Canada and Mexico was proposed by a meeting in San Antonio, Texas, in June 1991. It formed part of a series of regional free-trade agreements throughout North and South America – excluding only Cuba – that are intended to create a Free Trade Area of the Americas (FTAA). A summit in Quebec in April 2001 was called to set the agenda for the FTAA – and was met with massive protests. Resistance to it has grown across the continent. The summit in Mar del Plata, Argentina, in November 2005 failed to endorse the FTAA as the US Government, and some Latin American governments, had wanted.

NAFTA – which gives an indication of what the FTAA might eventually look like, if it is ever agreed – finally came into effect on 1 January 1994. It makes rules to remove 'distortions' and resolve trade disputes. It covers six broad areas:

● **Market access**: Average tariffs between Mexico, Canada and the US were already low, but high tariff barriers remained in the US and Canada against Mexican exports

● **Trade in services**: Deregulation of a broad range of commercial services, including finance and transport.

● **Foreign investment**: Prefiguring later, abandoned proposals for a Multilateral Agreement on Investment (MAI), NAFTA provides for 'national treatment' for all foreign investors.

● **Intellectual property**: Primarily a means of ensuring that patents held by corporations in the US or Canada are enforced in Mexico.

● **Dispute settlement**: This area was the most contentious, including the use of punitive sanctions and fines.

Virtually all the important concessions, on investment, intellectual property and services, were made by Mexico. ■

---

with the signing of NAFTA, an uprising would begin in Chiapas that continues to this day. It has become what the great Uruguayan writer Eduardo Galeano – a regular visitor – has styled 'the biggest siege in the world'. Once again, in Mexico City the people of Chiapas were derided, this time for seeking to make any connection at all between their obscure local difficulties and the grand designs of NAFTA.

A year or so later I came across José Juarez Varela from the Las Margaritas union office once again, this time in London. They had, he said, experienced an extremely difficult time; the uprising meant that they had lost one year's coffee harvest – a catastrophe. The Union had set up its own Café La Selva in a smart neighborhood of Mexico City, to sell their coffee and increase public awareness of their work. Fair and organic trade were even more important to them now, since their partners in the North had helped to keep them going through the disruption of the uprising and constant harassment by the Mexican military.

As for Mexico, within a year the country had been struck by a financial earthquake. An austerity program was imposed, destroying savings, cutting wages or throwing people out of work – so that Mexican banks could be bailed out of their misbegotten, NAFTA-related adventures. No such dispensation was offered to many thousands of small farmers who had taken the latest advice from the high priests of comparative advantage and borrowed heavily to invest in agricultural production for world markets.

Ciudad Juárez, for its part, is now notorious for industrial-scale criminal warfare of a quite shocking brutality, much of it directed against women. Which reminds me – Carlos Salinas, that elusive Harvard-educated President who knew so very well what was best for Mexico, who signed the NAFTA treaty but was never in his palace in the Zócalo, now lives in exile and disgrace. His brother was assassinated, but no doubt Salinas himself still has his hands on the fortune he made from oiling the works of the narcotics business. As for the PRI, it was finally ousted in the presidential elections of 2000 – by a former executive of Coca-Cola. Judge free trade by its results in Mexico and this is just about as good as it gets.

2 Coffee in Peru

What life is like for the first link in the chain of trade – the coffee farmers of the Tambopata river valley, on the border between Peru and Bolivia. How the coffee bean gets produced and why things never seem to work out.

IF TRADE IS a path, then fair trade is about the people it links together and who travel along it. Most paths carry an equal amount of traffic in both directions. The trade in coffee, like Southern commodities generally, is different. Large quantities of coffee beans arrive at their final destination with Northern consumers – but only a tiny trickle of cash ever returns to coffee farmers in the South.

There is something rather curious about this. If we were to measure the value of something by the amount of human intervention it receives, then by far the greatest value of the coffee bean would reside with the coffee farmer, whose working life is taken up with growing, picking, washing, drying and dispatching the thing. The very air is infused with the scent of fermenting coffee 'berries'. It's a safe bet that before it's consumed every single coffee bean will have been touched many times by the hands of a coffee farmer. Thereafter, hardly anyone will see it, let alone touch it. Yet the less they do so, the more likely they are to profit from it. You might imagine that we were talking here about two entirely different species – the one with eyes, hands and feet, the other with mystical powers and a metaphysical identity.

Coffee has been for some time the fastest-expanding fairly traded product. It now takes a sufficiently large chunk out of the conventional market to have an impact on it. In many respects it is the ideal fair-trade product, and therefore not entirely typical. It is a 'pure' commodity that requires no additions and relatively simple processing, so the fairness of the trade is relatively easy to assure. Small farmers account for a growing proportion of production – many of them own their land and work in co-operatives, thereby meeting one of the basic requirements of fair trade, though bearing also most of the risk. And the world market for coffee has become more fastidious, closer to wine, with specialty coffees increasingly popular at the expense of the bland, uniform blends – partly as a result of food scares in the North, and possibly even because fair trade is beginning to having some effect.

But that's all theory. Experience on the ground can look rather different.

'What has changed in my lifetime?' Abraham chuckled at the very idea. He was 73 years old in June 1995 when I talked to him in San Juan del Oro, an old town on the lower eastern slopes of the Peruvian Andes, in the valley of the great Tambopata River, which flows into the Amazon Basin. During the previous ten years, Abraham had lived through the crossfire of a civil war between Sendero Luminoso ('Shining Path') revolutionaries and the Peruvian Army. Peace was only just returning. I was curious to know what he made of it all.

'The *cafeteleros*, the coffee farmers,' he said, 'were poor when we came here 40 years ago, and we are just as poor now. That has not changed at all.'

Coffee in Peru

The earliest settlers here were Aymara- and Quechua-speaking peoples of the Peruvian Altiplano, who had lived for centuries around the desolate northern fringes of Lake Titicaca and were in urgent search of land. They began to 'make trouble', to form themselves into peasant unions. They were met with promises of reform. To relieve the pressure the Government built a road down into the forest that blankets the fragile, precipitous folds of the Andean escarpment to the east.

A new start

This was virgin territory, save for indigenous people retreating ever-deeper into the forest as the road advanced. Here there was space, fertile soil and an escape from the relentless cold of the Altiplano. The prospect of a better life was pursued by landless people believing that a good living might eventually be made from growing coffee.

But the bounty of this majestic forest is not easily won, and it is won hardest of all by destitute colonizers such as these with nothing but their own labor to invest. From the road durable paths had to be fashioned up the sheer sides of the mountains. The sites for settlement had to be carefully selected. The cold at levels higher than 2,625 feet (800 meters), the heat and humidity at levels lower than 650 feet (200 meters) above sea level would kill the coffee plant.

Gregorio Gomez lived further up the valley from San Juan del Oro. 'I was born in the Sierra, the mountains, near Sandia,' he told me. 'When I was less than a year old, my parents brought me here. They came because there was not much of a life to be had in the Sierra, and there were a lot of people. Here in the valley, in those days, there were few people but plenty of land and things to produce, especially coffee.

'So I took it upon myself to educate myself, what we call "auto-education". Many people here have to get an education in this way. I went to institutions in Juliaca and Puno on the Altiplano, getting jobs where I could earn my keep and pay the fees. But still I kept in touch with my parents here, and with the *chacra* (farm). In fact, I built my own, slightly apart from my parents' one.'

Edi, Gregorio's young nephew, lived there with them. Edi's mother (Gregorio's sister) had suffered terribly for a year from an illness that crept from her feet through her body until it killed her – at the age of 20. They never knew its name.

As well as Spanish, Gregorio spoke the Quechua language of the Altiplano. This put him in a minority – most people in the valley spoke Aymara. His family mostly lived elsewhere and he was the only one who remained to care for his parents, Luis and Celestina, in their old age.

He was a member of the small San Isidro coffee-producers' co-operative and had just been elected vice-president of CECOVASA, the central union of nine co-operatives in the region which co-ordinated the marketing of almost all its coffee production.

The coffee business

Gregorio farmed coffee because there was no other living he could make. He was at one end of an enormous international industry dedicated to satisfying the consuming passions of affluent Northern drinkers. That industry generates billion-dollar profits which the people who produce the coffee itself never see. Unless things change, they never will. Although they – like some 20 million others in the tropical countries of the South – have worked all their lives for coffee, coffee has not worked for them.

So I arranged to follow Gregorio in search of a straight answer to a very simple question. At the price of a cup of coffee in London or Toronto, Sydney or New York, the 110-pound (50 kilos) sacks of coffee beans he produced in the Tambopata Valley were worth something in the region of $13,000 each. Yet, if he was lucky, he and his co-operative received just $70. That's less than a 180th part.

Our first step along the way had to be upwards – quite a few steps upwards, to the steep, rainforest-coated slopes of the Tambopata River valley. It is hard to convey the sheer toil of climbing mountains through dense rainforest in humid tropical heat – something these farmers do all the time. Exhausted after just a few minutes, I stood bemused as a man scurried past me up the rough path, straining every sinew to push before him a wheelbarrow loaded with crates of Coca-Cola.

'Welcome to my *chacra*, my farm!' exclaimed Pamela when we eventually arrived, some two hours later. She took us by the hand and led us inside her house to a table decked with mandarins, papaya, jugs of juices, flowers, fresh herbs, simmering cups of cocoa. The one thing missing was coffee – if they drank it at all, the coffee farmers used it for relaxation in the afternoons.

'*Buenas tardes*, good afternoon,' said Pablo, Pamela's husband, after we had refreshed ourselves, introducing himself to my tape recorder. His darting eyes, mobile mouth and high-pitched croak made him seem roguish. But his laugh came straight from the soul.

'This is Pablo Cahuana Flores speaking. Member of the San Ignacio Co-operative. In the valley of the Tambopata River. Sandia. Department of Puno. Peru,' he shouted, as if reporting for duty. 'It is Friday.'

He trembled and was at a loss for words. More to the point, no outsiders – and certainly no gringos like me – had ever visited him on his *chacra* before. He waited for a while for the words to come, then seemed to conclude that the best way would be for us to see for ourselves. So he set off at high speed into the forest, beckoning us to follow and speaking fluently

Who gets what

In terms of the final price paid by consumers for a jar of coffee, by far the largest chunk stays in the North. Retailers (mostly supermarkets) have a 'mark-up' of around 25 per cent – a good bit lower than on some other lines, because the coffee market is large and 'price sensitive', which means consumers have traditionally been reluctant to pay more for what looks like a standard product.

The largest single chunk – 55 per cent – is taken by the shippers and roasters, a euphemism for the giant food corporations like Nestlé or Kraft General Foods which control three-quarters of the trade. A good part of this is used to promote the key brands, like Nescafé or Maxwell House. To preserve freshness, coffee beans tend to be blended, roasted, ground and (where necessary) processed into 'instant' granules close to the final consumer. Another ten per cent is taken by the exporters – the traders and dreaded 'middlemen' or coyotes who organize the trade in the producing country.

This leaves just ten per cent for the producers themselves. As a group, and in terms of the number of people involved, they receive far less than anyone else.

It is, of course, to them that fair trade is chiefly directed. But within current structures there is a limit on what can be achieved. The real costs of insurance, shipping, roasting and distribution remain much the same, if not higher for fair trade because it is relatively small-scale and therefore cannot extract the advantageous contracts given to the big corporations, or benefit equally from the economies of scale. ■

The coffee jar

Proportion received of the final price of a jar of coffee.

Growers 10%

Exporters 10%

COFFEE

Shippers and Roasters 55%

Retailers 25%

The Coffee Chain Game, Oxfam.

as he went.

The forest, he explained, had had to be thinned, while still preserving the shade needed by the coffee bushes, over an area of perhaps 7 acres (3 hectares) for each *chacra*. A platform had to be leveled to provide a drying area for the coffee, the loose soil soaked and compacted to form adobe walls for the two stories of the farmhouse; a building wide enough for a bed at each end, a table and bench in between, and not much else. A source of pure water had to be found. Finally, after the planting – first of essential vegetables and fruit for survival, then of the coffee itself – came the long, long wait: three years at least, tending the growing coffee plants 'like children' until the first fruits appeared. The hardships, the backbreaking labor without reward of these early years were still vivid in the memory of this place. They had never really gone away.

Forest product

'There they are,' he said, pointing to a clearing of felled trunks, forest litter and solitary papaya trees. A wooden aqueduct, perched on stilts, carried a trickle of water purposefully across the clearing into the forest beyond. Then I saw, nestling between two trunks, a bed of bright-green seedlings. 'They will serve me for 15 years,' said Pablo.

'Only 15?' I asked. The standard productive life of a coffee bush is more like 30 or 40 years.'That's right. Lower down they last a little longer. But they produce less coffee. Over there, those plants are two years old. Up there, three. When the flowers come out in September it is as if the mountains were covered in snow, just like the Altiplano.'

We entered a grove of mature coffee bushes. They were planted about two meters apart. Dappled gray, skeletal stems, several of them to a bush, fanned outwards from firm ground, clear and smooth save for a litter of leaves. The 'cherries', growing amid dark-green, glossy leaves from the stems of the outer fronds, turned from green to yellow and finally to red as they matured. They did, indeed, resemble small and unappetizing cherries. Interspersed among the coffee bushes were mandarin orange trees, brilliant with fruit.

Ahead we heard voices and there was Pamela again, beckoning frantically. She had draped a rough shawl from her shoulders to form two pouches around her waist. Half-a-dozen people, the men wearing numbered soccer shirts of the latest design, emerged from the bushes.

They were *peones*, laborers. They came down from the Altiplano for about five months every year during harvest time and lived in a shed beside the farmhouse. Every *chacra* employed *peones*. Around the valley, at intervals through the forest, precious level ground had been cleared for them to play soccer on Sundays. They called Pamela and Pablo *dueños*, owners. There was, however, little to distinguish between them in terms of their apparent wealth.

The pace of events began to quicken. Coffee cherries flew in all directions. Mandarin oranges were plucked from the trees – a sack of 100 sold for less than one US dollar on local markets. There were bouts of hilarity as Pamela and her band of *peones* gave an exuberant exhibition of their daily drudgery.

Harvest time

This was harvest time for coffee – a critical time of year for the entire community, on which its fate for the coming year hinged. Pablo was keen to impress upon me the seriousness of the task. 'We also produce coffee here for the *comercio alternativo*, for fair trade. We are careful to select only the best cherries for them, the ones that are perfectly ripe. It is a risk for us. There is only one day when they are perfect. If it rains on that day then they fall from the bushes and are lost. Sometimes it has rained for weeks during the harvest.'

The pouches were filled with cherries and we descended again towards the *chacra*. To one side of the farmhouse the wooden aqueduct poured crystal-clear water into a concrete tank. A vessel resembling a fat dugout canoe was filled with water. The cherries were unloaded into it and floated on the surface. They would sink slowly to the bottom as they fermented.

Beside this vessel was another similar one, filled previously, from which the fermented cherries were now removed and spread out to dry for a few hours. These cherries, by now reeking of fermenting fruit – a scent that remains with the coffee beans and I can smell to this day – were passed through a crude but effective de-pulper. Pour the cherries into a hopper at the top, rotate the handle and hey presto! the soft fruit pulp falls out to one side while the hard coffee beans clatter down a tin chute to the other. The pulp would eventually be returned to the soil as compost. The beans still had a thick and resistant mucus coating. They were passed through more fresh water at least five or six times and literally scrubbed by foot or by hand. It was an extremely laborious process.

The drying process

The result – beans shining like polished peanuts – is called *café lavado*, washed coffee. These beans were spread out to dry in the sun for two or three days. Beans for the 'normal' market were placed on black synthetic material stretched directly over the ground. The *comercio alternativo* beans were on raised wooden platforms so that air could pass beneath them, making the drying process more effective. If rain threatened – and every night – the beans had to be gathered in and kept dry.

A husk still remained on the beans. Pamela and

Pablo tested them as the drying proceeded by rubbing them between their hands to remove the husk and inspect the color and texture of the bean inside, until there was no sign of moisture and it had taken on a particular shade of gray-green. In this condition, still covered with the husk and known as *café pergamino*, the beans can be preserved for long periods without deteriorating – a quality that allows coffee to be produced as a cash crop even in such isolated spots as this.

We convened into a small circle to consider the implications of what we had seen. Gregorio conducted the interviews. We had been joined by Octavio Morales, a thin, solemn neighbor immaculately dressed and wearing a flat cloth cap.

'*Señor periodista inglés*,' Octavio began slowly in a deep, resonant and mournful voice, addressing me, the English journalist. 'We send greetings to your compatriots so far away and ask them to keep drinking their coffee. We want to thank you for coming to visit us here, the first journalist we have ever seen. Now you know for yourself how we must live, what a labor it is to produce coffee. But on the New York Coffee Exchange this morning the price has fallen to just $143 a sack.'

I was a little incredulous. How cold he possibly have known that?

'Yes,' continued Pablo, before I had a chance to ask. 'The price does not adequately reflect the work we put in, the costs we have to pay to maintain our families, employ *peones* and everything else. We produce coffee here of the highest quality, without using chemical fertilizers, herbicides or fungicides. Our coffee is completely organic and should receive a better price.'

I made a few simple calculations in my head. Assume that Pamela and Pablo would receive the equivalent of about $70 dollars, after the deduction of transport and processing costs, for each 110-pound

(50 kilos) sack of *café pergamino* they were eventually able to sell – a pretty good price. If their *chacra* totaled about three hectares, and two hectares actually produced coffee at a good average (for here) of 20 sacks per hectare (10,000 sq km or 2.5 acres), then they should have been able sell a total of 40 sacks and receive a gross income of some $2,800. Scarcely a princely reward, but still not far off the average income in Peru. However, out of this sum they still had to pay the wages and keep of the *peones* and the cost of transport by mule to the nearest coffee store. More to the point, three years previously they had received less than $20 per sack. Such prices were typical of the years between 1989 and 1993, when their income did not even cover the costs of production. The year before, after frost had killed part of the coffee crop in Brazil, a sack had sold for as much as $200 – a bonanza for Pamela and Pablo.

Survival mechanisms

To understand what this kind of uncertainty means for them, however, you have first to realize that the difference is not just between 'good' and 'bad' times. It's not so much a question of whether you have enough to eat – the forest is just about bountiful enough to make malnutrition avoidable. But, if your coffee harvest brings you in less than it costs you, if you have labored for a year without reward, then you will have nothing to pay for treatment for you or your children when sickness strikes, as it invariably does in places such as this – yellow fever is rampant. As a result, there are no doctors or medicines. The prevailing certainty then is that if you get really sick you die – it's as simple as that. Whether or not you will be able to keep your children in school is doubtful. So there are not enough schools. The cumulative effect of all this continuing year after year, and of having to submit your life entirely to the whims of world coffee prices, is what powerlessness really means.

It also means that you take your chance to celebrate when you can. So our leaving ceremony became extremely protracted – suddenly everyone was equipped with compact cameras, bought with the bounty of the previous year's bonanza. We lined up by the *chacra*, by the drying coffee beans, the pulping machines, the coffee bushes and the papaya trees; we embraced different combinations of *peones*, *dueños*, families, friends, enemies, children and lovers, and we satisfied that universal longing to have our portraits made. Strange that I felt at all uneasy at leaving mine, my own 'soul', behind in this place – when I thought nothing of taking theirs with me.

We set off into the forest. We had been going just 15 minutes when we were stopped at a promontory by Daniel Limarche, who kept a shop. Inside was a cornucopia for sale: tinned fish, rice, Coca-Cola and a dozen bottles of real champagne. Daniel took me to a house where his niece was waiting, seated on a chair – a waif of a girl aged about seven. Her parents stood on each side of her. Daniel asked me if I would be her *padrino*, her godfather. He gave me a pair of scissors and asked me to cut off her hair – it would remain as a memento. Little Isabel began to weep as I cut her wispy strands.

The path descended in zigzags across the slopes of the valley. Giant trees stood over us; streams tumbled through dark, shaded air and the forest animals called their warnings – a sudden sound like a large drop of water falling into a still pond, or a slowly descending, derisive jeer. Out over the valley a condor glided patiently by. Treading a path where the stones had been worn smooth by the passage of human feet, we crossed sections that had been entirely swept away, the forest replaced by tangled roots, ugly naked earth baking dry and dusty in the sunlight – giant landslides. Some of them were still moving as we crossed.

The price is wrong

The price for Robusta beans is fixed largely on the London Commodity Exchange; for the milder Arabica beans largely on the New York Commodity Exchange.

All sorts of things determine what that price is. There is, of course, 'supply' – the amount of beans available. The more there are, the lower the price will be. Then there is 'demand', or the amount of coffee people want to consume. The more of that there is, the higher the price will be. Since demand for coffee has been growing steadily, you'd have thought its price would have been rising. In fact it's been falling.

That's partly because more bushes get planted by farmers when prices start to rise, – but they don't start producing for three years, when there's a glut and prices fall. Occasionally a natural event will restrict supply and prices will rise sharply. Two things characterize the world price of coffee. The first is a dramatic variation from year to year, even day to day, making it very difficult for producers to plan ahead. One reason for this is speculation. Some coffee is bought on 'futures' markets or as a 'hedge' against these kinds of fluctuations. This is supposed to 'stabilize' the market – in fact it does just the reverse, since speculators 'play' this market and shift large sums of money around very quickly.

The second characteristic is a long-term decline in the price of coffee. Unlike oil producers, coffee-producing countries do not work together to control production and therefore force prices up. The governments of these countries used to make agreements of this kind, but these collapsed in 1989. Periodic attempts to revive them have so far met with little success. ■

Casino café

Frost damaged the Brazilian coffee crop in 1994, causing prices to rise. The overall trend is downwards amid sharp fluctuations from year to year and month to month.

January average of International Coffee Organization Indicator price, US cents per pound.

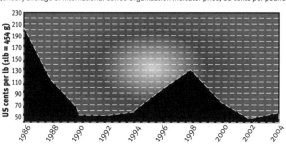

International Coffee Organization.

It was tempting to push the ecological alarm button. This is an extremely sensitive environment – the headwaters of the Amazon. Four years previously I had been in the Brazilian Amazon just to the north, where concern had been mounting for some time at the increased rate that silt was being carried down into the Amazon Basin from the Peruvian escarpment, with unpredictable and possibly catastrophic environmental consequences throughout the region.

Fragile environment

Blaming the coffee colonists for this looked, at first sight, like a fairly straightforward matter. They were, after all, thinning the forest, weakening the delicate structures that hold a thin layer of topsoil to the slopes. Coffee is, like cash crops generally, a voracious consumer of the limited nutrients in the soil. All it takes is heavy rain and the soil erodes.

But the matter was not as simple as this. The whole of this region is, in geological terms, a very young environment, still in the process of formation. The soil of the Amazon rainforest itself derives largely from the silt eroded from these mountains; at least some is needed to replenish what is constantly washed into the Atlantic Ocean by the natural action of the giant river system. Looking to the summits of the mountains you could see light-green, healing scars made by earlier landslides caused quite naturally by rain, lightning strikes or earth tremors.

What was not in doubt, however, was that the colonists were accelerating the natural process. They knew this well enough, losing as they did with every rainfall some of the fertility on which they relied for their very lives. Higher up the valley they told me that temperatures had begun to fall as the forest thinned – just as they had fallen in Brazil, which was why the Brazilian coffee crop had been affected by frost and the previous year's 'bonanza' had happened here.

Coffee in Peru

No less in doubt was that it did not have to be this way. For the coffee colonists operated, as they had always done, without any support or technical assistance of any kind. You did not have to be an expert – as I am not – to conclude that the most minimal precautions, such as terracing or a more informed approach to the thinning of the tree-cover, could have had a beneficial effect.

The problem was that people already on the brink knew that this, more even than healthcare or education, was beyond their means. There was no point whatever in advocating such things unless the resources were there to achieve them. Forty years of working for the conventional coffee trade had not produced these resources: no-one believed that it ever would. So everyone kept silent, hurrying without comment across the landslides, fearing perhaps that some eco-imperialists might manage to banish them from their precious land altogether.

Since then Conservation International has arrived from the US and begun what might eventually result in just that. A project is underway to create a 'buffer' zone between the coffee farmers and the nature reserve in the Tambopata River Basin.

If I were a coffee farmer I might well be wondering why such palliatives must always arrive as unfamiliar offerings – with yet more instructions – from the source of the injustice itself, leaving my basic predicament intact. I'd be working for the day when I and my community had the power to decide for ourselves; I'd know for certain that, in the long run and for my children's children, this is the only kind of change that works.

The long road to market

With disconcerting abruptness we emerged from the dimness of the forest path into brilliant light shimmering from the surface of a rough, dirt road. On the outer lip of the road an arc of tin-roofed, wooden huts perched over a precipice. A line of people sat in the shade on wooden benches watching the world, the coffee, an ancient bus, a small truck sprouting people like a vase, clatter by.

They called this place Punta de la Carretera, 'end of the road'. But this was just the beginning of the long, long voyage our coffee had yet to make to meet its market. An hour or so along the road was a rare sight, a large area of gently sloping ground and an expanse of tin roofs shining in the sun. This was Putina Punco, the first settlement of any real size – about 20,000 people – and the center for the coffee farmers of the Tambopata Valley. From here we visited *chacras* belonging to all four co-operatives – two big ones, San Jorge and Charuyo, with more than a thousand members each; two small ones, San Ignacio and Union Azata.

Coffee prices by radio

Near the river was a concrete square surrounded by warehouses. The co-op members brought their sacks here from great distances by mule – sometimes even on their backs – to be weighed, tested for quality, registered, stored and dispatched in large Volvo trucks. From an office to one side came the sound of a short-wave radio powered by a solar cell linked to a car battery. The *cafeteleros* could talk directly to Lima and learn the price of coffee that very moment on the New York Coffee Exchange. So that was where flat-capped Octavio had got the coffee price before we spoke on the farm earlier in the day.

One small co-op, the Union Azata, had lost a large chunk of its membership, which had once stood at 800 and was then no more than 120. *Chacras* had been abandoned, the investment lost, during the lean years between 1989 and 1993. Gregorio told me that Putina Punco had become a ghost town, losing 70 per cent of its population.

'Please tell your readers, so far away on other continents,' said Hugo, a young and very bright official of Union Azata, 'that thousands of people here in this valley depend on the coffee they buy. You have seen how things are; how hard, how very hard we try to produce coffee of good quality for them. Tell them that we receive minimal payment for all our efforts. And tell all those ecologists, those very distinguished professionals, tell them to come and visit us here. Tell them that our forests are being extinguished and that we urgently, urgently need their help.'

'What we faced before the co-ops were founded,' added Gregorio, 'was having to sell all our coffee to a few powerful *comerciantes*, intermediaries. They committed a kind of violence against us. They treated coffee just like anything else, with ruthless self-interest and indifference to its quality, and the price they paid was very low.

'That didn't suit us. It didn't suit us at all. It was a very difficult struggle and we had to make many sacrifices, building our own warehouses, our own communications, transport and so on. However low the price of coffee may fall, we shall maintain our Co-op to the last, after all the sacrifices we made to set it up.'

I found the sheer isolation of this place intimidating. Sometimes I lay awake at night and it played on my mind. If it had rained at all heavily we would have been completely cut off, possibly for weeks. There was no electricity, no medicine, not a single doctor. Yellow fever stalked the houses. So it was with some initial relief that I set off along the road out of Putina Punco taken by the coffee trucks.

We wound our way up the valley, climbing all the while. We stopped off at San Juan del Oro again, a slightly larger and older version of Putina Punco, with a gold mine in the mountains above, where Gregorio would work when times were bad with coffee. We filled the Nissan with petrol siphoned from barrels piled high in a store. An old man took me to see his run-down *chacra*, asserting repeatedly: 'What we need is technology!' Further along the road we called in at Gregorio's San Isidro co-op in Yanahuaya, then left him at his parents' *chacra*, where he had work to do on the coffee harvest.

Onto the Altiplano

And so, eventually, we set off for the Altiplano. As we climbed, the forest gave way to scrub and then arid rubble. The higher we climbed the more the mountains seemed to loom over us, the more precipitous became the fall to the river ever-further below us. At the head of one valley was an amphitheater of astonishing grandeur, terraces cut into the side of the mountain by the Incas and still used to carry the weight of the road, which zigzagged straight upwards. It proved wise not to look over the edge, as if from an aircraft, at the receding pins of light in the deepening dusk on the valley floor. This, I was told, was where *cafetelero* Abraham had lost one of his sons.

The cold became intense, penetrating, as darkness engulfed us. With the altitude my breathing began to labor, my head to spin and ache, the pain amplified by violent blows against the side and roof of the lurching vehicle, which I was helpless to prevent. We could see nothing except the dusty track ahead, illuminated in the head lamps. I envied the inanimate coffee bean that came this way too.

We stopped at what at first appeared to be a bright doorway in space. Slowly, as my eyes adjusted to the radiant starlight, I could see the shadows of buildings and, behind them, snow peaks near enough to touch. The summit of the pass. We had climbed for six hours, from 800 to 5,000 meters, more than 16,000 feet above sea level.

The journey was still far from over, though we climbed no more. I recall a reflection of stars dancing on the surface of Lake Titicaca, and a bright strip of orange light in the distance – Juliaca, our destination and the end of the stars. After a day and a night on the road, dawn was not far away.

Juliaca is built from the materials of the earth on which it stands and it was not always easy to tell whether the buildings were rising up from it or subsiding back into it. The streets were jammed with rickshaws and markets. The town had two great attractions for the coffee producers: electricity to drive a processing plant and banks for the export business.

So it was here that the Central Office of Agrarian Coffee-producing Co-operatives of the Valleys of Sandia (CECOVASA) had its base. The coffee trucks from Putina Punco arrived in the yard and unloaded their cargo into a warehouse. At the end of the warehouse was a line of green machines made in Brazil and Colombia. The first shook out the crudest impurities in the *café pergamino*: stones, wood and other relics of the valleys. From here the bean passed into a cylindrical mill which removed its husk – and, I was later to discover, a good part of its taste as well. Pergamin coffee beans are not uniform and the husks are liable to more rapid decay than the beans, so are not what world markets require. Finally, the naked bean emerged; a small, unprepossessing lozenge in two fused segments known as 'green' coffee.

Export grading

A stack of four more sieves, shaking violently, graded the green beans by size. Only the largest were considered suitable for export – as in most coffee-exporting countries, inferior beans were sold for domestic consumption only. Something like 20 per cent of the beans failed to pass muster for export. Finally they ran the gauntlet of a conveyor belt set between a line of hired hands who completed a manual grading process, leaving only beans akin to jewels.

The previous year CECOVASA had exported almost

22,000 sacks of green coffee, valued at some $3.5 million. Until the early 1980s all coffee exports from Peru had to go through government agencies, which had traditionally relied on the US market. Since then – and with a marked improvement in the doubtful reputation for quality of Peruvian beans – new markets had been developed in Japan and Europe, which now bought 80 per cent of their coffee.

'We have good news,' said Pablo, the manager, sitting in an office with fair-trade posters covering the walls. 'The price is rising. Over $150 on the New York Exchange today. Rumors of another poor harvest in Brazil. An announcement expected from the Brazilian Government shortly. This is a relief for us. We have been holding on, waiting to make sales because we thought the price would rise – but instead it fell.'

The green coffee now had to travel in rented 20-ton trucks for two days across a mountainous desert down to the coast, then north to Callao, Lima's seaport. Time, graciously, insisted that I fly from Juliaca to Lima. In Callao an official in a sharp black uniform plunged a stiletto blade into some of the sacks as they arrived, searching for cocaine. No-one had said much about it – and I had not asked – but everyone clearly knew well enough that when the coffee trade slumped the coca trade flourished. A gang of laborers lined a container with brown paper and filled it with 250 sacks to make up the standard 'lot'. The doors were sealed. The beans would not see the light of day again until they reached their destination; through the Panama Canal to Europe or North America; across the Pacific to Japan and Australasia. I gave them a friendly pat to see them on their way. Meanwhile, the coffee price in New York fell.

3 Cocoa in Ghana

How much cocoa means to Ghana and the people who produce it. What 'structural adjustment' or 'poverty reduction' policies do in practice, not least to the cocoa farmers themselves. Why the gains they've made from being able to organize have been lost in other ways.

A COMMON FEATURE of many Southern countries is that they depend very heavily indeed on a single export crop. Even a huge and relatively wealthy country like Brazil relied until quite recently on a sequence of single export commodities, shifting in turn from sugar to rubber to coffee and soy beans, but never sustaining them together so that bad years in one might be balanced out by better years in another. One reason for this is the way 'comparative advantage' on world markets makes one crop temporarily very much more profitable than another, thereby encouraging a herd instinct – particularly in powerful landowners – to switch en masse between them and promoting extremely vulnerable 'monoculture' economies.

Another aspect of this phenomenon relates less to abstract theories of 'comparative advantage' than to the past, since the economies of colonies were constructed to suit the colonial power. Whether it was cotton from India, spices from Southeast Asia, gold from South Africa or cocoa from Ghana, the 'value' of these commodities was conceived entirely in Northern terms, with little regard to the long-term benefits or otherwise to local people.

From this it has followed that the economic 'spread effect' – bringing greater prosperity to the population as a whole – of commodity exporting has always been extremely limited. By and large, the value that is added to a basic raw material by its processing, manufacture and commercialization has been retained very firmly in the North – and with it the capital for future development. The advent of independence has done little to alter the basic shape of this process. Particularly in Africa, many countries remain as dependent today on a single export crop as they were in colonial times.

The consequences of this reach deep into post-colonial societies. Not least, their governments rely very heavily on taxing exports to generate revenues. This consolidates the political influence of the world trading system over these societies, whether they have achieved self-determination and political independence or not.

In recent years the political impact of this economic relationship has been made more overt by the debt crisis. Northern creditors have been able to insist not merely on repayment, but on precisely how the economies of debtor countries are to be run. Their prescription, 'structural adjustment' or 'poverty reduction', has become entirely formulaic: the promotion of exports, the devaluation of currencies to make exports even cheaper, the removal of regulations, the withdrawal of democratic control, the cutting of public expenditure on basic services like education and healthcare, the privatization of public assets: in short, the neoliberal agenda.

It is now becoming clear that this agenda has failed. To get an idea of how and why, NI editor Richard Swift took a closer look at cocoa in Ghana. This is what he found.

Out in the field

Heat and light begin to settle over Accra before six in the morning. It is the kind of heat where the cotton of your shirt already sticks to your skin by eight in the morning... and you search for a breath of breeze blowing off the Atlantic. I have arranged with Sam Nyako of the Ghanaian Cocobod (cocoa marketing board) to travel upcountry to the Cocoa Research Institute in Tafo and to the Agricultural College which trains the board's extension officers, who help farmers improve their cocoa production. It will give me a chance to have a look at what Ghana does to sustain a crop that is a vital part of its economic well-being. Also, to find out firsthand about the effects of the economic liberalization process, designed with World Bank and International Monetary Fund (IMF) help, that is having a dramatic impact not only on cocoa farmers but on all Ghanaians.

Accra is just waking up as we pull out of town and start the journey towards Tafo, a town located in the upcountry, about four hours' drive to the northeast. The combination of the cooler height and the breeze blowing in through the window of the four-wheel-drive provides welcome relief. As we climb we are treated to a spectacular view of the Accra plain spread out below, the shimmering Atlantic beyond. Long lines of school children in brown tunics, pants and neat yellow shirts stretch out along the road all the way to the next hilltop. They meander past Ghana's 'informal sector' setting itself up on the roadside to sell anything it has that anyone could conceivably want, or afford, to buy: huge yams, *fou fou* (porridge), soups (the Ghanaian name for stews, or indeed almost any food), toilet paper, batteries, pens, lottery tickets – you name it.

As we drive north Sam fills me in on the history of the Ghanaian Cocobod. It has its roots in the colonial buying monopoly set up by the British at the time of the Second World War. This was in response to African complaints that they were getting ripped off by the expatriate firms whose agents monopolized the purchase of the cocoa crop. The early history of cocoa production here is marked by a series of struggles in which farmers got together to hold back the sale of their crops and force up the price.

While the declared purpose of the board was to shield farmers from speculators and price fluctuations, it never in fact did this. For the British, and later for independent Ghanaian Governments, cocoa proved too tempting a source of public finance to allow a fair price. Proceeds from cocoa had to underwrite the plans of Kwame Nkrumah for ambitious education, health and industrial projects. So heavy export taxes and other tariffs kept producer prices low. 'We compensated for this at the Cocobod, at least partially,' Sam Nyako says, 'by a series of free services to farmers, including subsidized fertilizers, pesticides and herbicides, free agricultural extension services, research and development of the best cocoa hybrids for Ghanaian conditions, free saplings, even labor to help at busy times on the farm.' The argument was that despite low prices farmers were getting back some value in services.

Market fluctuations

But this did not prove enough to sustain the cocoa economy. When the bottom first dropped out of the cocoa market in the 1970s (as it did more recently in 1999-2000), prices tumbled from almost $4,800 a ton to less than a third of that. With farmers getting less than 40 per cent of the world price from the Cocobod, this was a significant blow. Many farmers stopped producing cocoa altogether or switched to food crops like maize and cassava that fetched more reliable prices.

The situation worsened with the Sahelian drought that hit West Africa in the early 1980s. By 1983 conditions were so dry that a series of disastrous bush fires swept across Ghana's cocoa-growing country. Production plummeted. In 1972 Ghana produced nearly a third of the world's cocoa. A decade later this had fallen to just 12 per cent. With Ghana, like most of sub-Saharan Africa, staggering under a huge debt burden, the collapse of cocoa left the country teetering on the edge of bankruptcy.

It was at this point that the World Bank and IMF stepped in with a structural-adjustment package to 'rescue' the country's economy. If you read all the official literature you will conclude that this has been a tremendous success. For cocoa this meant a dramatically downsized Cocobod and significantly higher prices for farmers. All sounds like good stuff.

As we pull through the gates of the Cocoa Research Institute in Tafo I get an idea of the effort that has been made to sustain vital cocoa yields. The station dates from colonial times and has a range of laboratories, experimental farms, nurseries and so many PhDs that Sam jokingly refers to them as 'doctors without nurses'. It concentrates on basic plant science, with special attention to cocoa as a small-farmer crop. It has pioneered inter-cropping, allowing small farmers to grow food crops in the three-to-five years it takes cocoa trees to produce their first pods.

At Tafo they have developed a hybrid cocoa, marrying the traditional type to a new Amazonian variety from Brazil with an eye to taste, bean count, yield per acre (0.405 hectares), disease resistance and quickness to maturity. The old type yields only one crop after five years whereas the new variety yields two crops after just three years – a vital difference for marginal small farmers. The Institute feels their hybrid is the most productive for West African conditions.

We move from building to building meeting with the plant people, the bug people, the disease people, the cocoa byproducts division and finally the economist. It quickly becomes clear that, while the Institute has been vital in sustaining cocoa as a small-farmer crop, there is a constant tension between its expensive, scientific, agrochemical approach and what the farmers can afford to do in the field.

We drive to the Cocobod's Agricultural College at

Bunso. Here the mood is decidedly more downbeat. Structural-adjustment reforms have bitten deep into the agricultural extension service. Overall, the Cocobod has dropped from some 100,000 employees to less than 10,000. In areas like extension the effects

---

Chocolate follies – a brief history

The first known use of the cocoa bean was to make a spicy (not sweet) chocolate drink and dates back to the Mayan empire (250-900AD) in what is today southern Mexico and Guatemala. It was a symbol of sanctity and evoked both fertility and prosperity. Thence it spread to the Aztec Empire to the North, where beans were also used as currency. Chocolate was not immediately to the taste of the Spanish conquistadores, until sugar was added to accommodate the passion of Europeans for sweetness. They made chocolate into a tablet that was readily transportable to Europe. The fanatical Charles the Second of Spain reportedly sat sipping chocolate while observing victims of the Inquisition being put to death.

For some time chocolate remained a mysterious luxury item largely confined to the Iberian peninsular in Europe. Slowly it spread with trade across the continent. Experts debated whether it cooled over-heated or heated cooler passions. The Marquis de Sade's status as one of the earliest-known 'chocoholics' added a certain spice to its reputation.

With the invention of the cocoa press by the Dutchman Van Houten in the late 19th century, cocoa butter could be extracted from the beans, leaving a powder of cocoa solids. A vast new confectionery industry came into being. The Cadbury company brought the press to England and was quickly joined by Rowntree, together with Milton Hershey and then Forest E Mars in the United States.

Today, less than two per cent of cocoa comes from Mexico. World production shifted to West Africa at the end of the 19th century. The belief in Ghana is that the cocoa seedlings were smuggled in by a Ghanaian carpenter named Tetteh Quarshie in 1878. Ghana was the world's largest producer between 1910 and 1979.

Chocolate companies, buyers and development agencies like the World Bank encouraged a number of new countries to begin producing the 'miracle' commodity. Asian countries like Malaysia and Indonesia set up large plantations, while Brazil and other Latin American countries also increased their production. The result was an increase in supply – and a fall in price. Most of the plantations have not, however, been a success and Malaysia is withdrawing from the market. Plantations are still rare in West Africa. ∎

have been dramatic. Workloads have doubled and Alfred Nortley, one of the College's administrators, reports that 'morale is low. It is almost impossible to do your job, and the farmers are starting to complain quite bitterly.' The College is not currently training extension workers at all as there are simply no jobs. This may also explain the frustration back at the Institute. It is the extension workers who are charged with transferring the Institute's agronomy on to the farmers.

Cuts at Cocobod

No-one would seriously argue there was no fat in the Cocobod and cuts weren't needed. Many of its workers and functions were of marginal utility and at the cost of a better price to cocoa farmers. Today the price farmers get has risen to 50 per cent of the international price, with the Board committed to go even higher, to 65 or 70 per cent. But structural adjustment is turning out to be a blunt instrument, cutting away many of the beneficial services to farmers the Cocobod did perform. Put this together with the other effects of structural adjustment and it is by no means clear that cocoa farmers – supposedly one of the main beneficiaries of the IMF/World Bank reforms – are much better off. Not only are inputs more expensive, but the cost of living for ordinary Ghanaians has skyrocketed. In all my time in Ghana I never heard anyone say anything positive about the impact of structural adjustment.

As we head back towards Accra my conversation with Sam shifts to other changes in the farmers' lives. The user fees in education and health have been particularly difficult. There are lots of stories about those who simply can't afford schooling. For most, higher education is inconceivable. Sam is particularly aware of the effects on health costs. He recounts stories of people turned away from hospitals in the middle of the night, forced to carry desperately sick family members back home either because they lacked the money or just because the banks were closed and they couldn't get their hands on the cash. Sam shakes his head and stares out of the window pensively. The words come slowly. 'Ghana never used to be like this,' he says.

To help shore up public revenues and meet Ghana's obligations to international creditors, as well as cover the high cost of imports resulting from the devalued *cedi*, the IMF/World Bank package called for a value-added tax (VAT) to replace all other sales taxes. The idea was to shift some of the tax burden away from cocoa and encourage production. But when the Government tried to bring in the tax at 17 per cent even the usually peaceful Ghanaians took to the streets in protest. They cried '*kume preko*' ('kill me quickly' – as opposed to the lingering death of structural adjustment) and the police obliged, gunning down several demonstrators. But the outcry was so great that the Government was forced to back down.

The cocoa co-op
The headquarters of Kuapa Kokoo (cocoa co-op), is in the Ashante capital of Kumasi – Ghana's second-largest city and the heart of cocoa country. Its offices occupy the two floors of a large villa-like building. The number of comings and goings is a good hint that this is where a lot of the cocoa action in town takes place. Despite the obvious busyness, this is no stuffy office. Cocoa farmers sit around chatting, and some have spent the night on the floor of a large sleeping room: testament to the comfort and sense of ownership of Kuapa members.

Kuapa has several faces. It is at once a farmers' union, a cocoa-purchasing company and a trust fund for its members. It started back in 1993 when Nana Frimpong Abebrese, a far-sighted farmers' representative on Cocobod, saw that the partial privatization of internal purchase might leave cocoa farmers at the mercy of unscrupulous private companies. He feared a return to the bad old days when middlemen-buyers and moneylenders preyed on farmers. The best way to avoid this, he surmised, was for the farmers to organize themselves to collect, sell and profit from their own cocoa. To do this the union had to set up its own purchasing company, as under Ghanaian company law it was illegal for a co-operative to buy and sell cocoa without a license from the Cocobod.

How it works

A local society is the basic building block of Kuapa and can vary from dozens to hundreds of members. When it started, Kuapa had 22 local societies – the number mushroomed to 160 in 1998. Today, Kuapa is operational in 26 areas, with around 1,200 village societies and 45,000 farmer members. The proportion of women farmers has grown from 13 per cent to nearly 30 per cent. Kuapa Kokoo relies on committed and energetic staff. The current head of the Gender and Society Development activities is a woman, Anna Antwi, who barely mentions the cocoa-chemistry degree and training in cocoa agronomy that lies behind her work with her department, which passionately advocates community organization, good meeting practices, women's rights and support activities.

Blending the desirable and the necessary is crucial for a fledgling grassroots organization such as Kuapa, which needs to avoid becoming a voice in the wilderness or falling into business-as-usual cronyism. Support workers spend a good deal of time on the road strengthening existing societies or establishing new ones. Most Kuapa Kokoo workers appear to balance a commitment to the cocoa farmers' cause with caution born of the realization of the importance

Trade and development – no automatic link

Orthodox economics suggest that the more a country trades – and in particular, exports – the greater the well-being of its people. Even by traditional measures, like economic growth, this is far from always being true. In 1997, for example, Russian exports (mostly of commodities like oil) were growing rapidly but its economy grew by just 0.4 per cent. Meanwhile, wages fell by almost half in that year alone, after seven years during which inequality had doubled and male life expectancy declined by more than four years. The trade wealth disappeared into the pockets of an élite (much of it criminal) plugged into the circuits of economic globalization.

Taking broader measures of human development, the picture is no less ambiguous. The UN's Development Program (UNDP) has a 'human development index' (HDI) which includes broader measures of well-being – education, health, gender, inequality – than mere money. It goes on to suggest what level of well-being might reasonably be expected from the material wealth of a particular society. Some relatively poor societies – like the Indian state of Kerala – achieve much higher levels of well-being than might be expected, while some relatively rich ones – like Saudi Arabia or Switzerland – achieve very much less. For these latter there is a 'shortfall' on the HDI, which characterizes several societies around the world.

Combining three measures of development – exports, average income and the HDI shortfall – showed when they were studied in the late 1980s and early 1990s (see chart) wide variations. In some places, like Singapore and Mauritius, strong growth in exports corresponds with rapid growth in incomes and marked reductions in the HDI shortfall. In others, like Pakistan or Uganda, exports and incomes have grown quite quickly but the HDI shortfall has been reduced very little.

The reasons for this are associated above all with government policies and political decisions. ∎

Trade, growth and well-being 1985-97 (per cent)

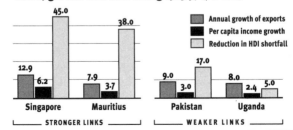

Annual growth of exports
Per capita income growth
Reduction in HDI shortfall

	Singapore	Mauritius	Pakistan	Uganda
Annual growth of exports	12.9	7.9	9.0	8.0
Per capita income growth	6.2	3.7	3.0	2.4
Reduction in HDI shortfall	45.0	38.0	17.0	5.0

STRONGER LINKS — WEAKER LINKS

Human Development Report 1999, UNDP.

of the annual crop to the whole country. Nana Anson, a former Society Development Officer, is clear: 'Ghana has developed on the back of the cocoa farmer: roads, hospitals, schools, everything comes from cocoa.'

It is ironic that it is the structural-adjustment program, so unpopular throughout Ghana, that has given the space for Kuapa to exist. It forced the Cocobod to give up its monopoly on internal purchase, allowing the farmers themselves to take over this function. The Cocobod has technically kept its word: producer prices are rising as a share of the market price beyond 55 per cent or even the 60 per cent promised. But, while farmers are enthusiastic for increased prices, all workers in the sector are cautious about the total liberalization of cocoa marketing being pushed by the World Bank and the IMF.

What happens elsewhere

Other countries in West Africa, such as Cameroon, Nigeria and to a lesser extent Côte d'Ivoire, that are opening up cocoa purchase and export to external companies, have suffered a perilous deterioration in quality, worsening prices and a rush for quick profit. 'Ghana produces the best cocoa in the world and we get a premium on the price. It is the Cocobod's Quality Control Division that is largely responsible for maintaining these standards,' cautions Nana Anson. He is also quick to underline other deleterious effects of adjustment policies on farmers, such as the collapse of a once-vital rural-credit system due to imposed reforms. Most farmers can no longer meet the stringent criteria for collateral demanded by the banks and end up either without vital credit or borrowing from private moneylenders and purchasing companies at rates of up to 100-per-cent interest.

It is not hard to figure out the attraction of Kuapa for Ghana's cocoa farmers. Not only do they run their own show, but it's a much better deal. For the last three years in a row, with other new companies barely trading, Kuapa paid a bonus to every farmer averaging 500 *cedis* per bag over and above the Cocobod price. An additional 300 *cedis* per bag went into the coffers of the local village societies for their own work and activities. At the end of the year, four representatives from each society – two women and two men – come to Kumasi for a big meeting to divide up the year's profits. In the last two years this has amounted to 700 cedis per bag. This is a matter of a few US cents and may seem like small potatoes – but for a hard-pressed farmer it can make a big difference.

Between 2 and 4 per cent of Kuapa's output is sold to fair-trade organizations in Europe – these include the Day Chocolate Company and the Body Shop (now owned by L'Oréal), which uses fair-trade cocoa butter in its line of natural cosmetics. The British-based organization, Twin Trading, helps orchestrate these arrangements. However, they are by no means assured, as I learn when I meet the Managing Director of the marketing company. He expresses some fear that fair-trade organizations may not buy the full amount of cocoa that Kuapa has allotted for them this year.

Fair traders

On what they do purchase, these fair-traders return a premium to Kuapa which is based on a minimum price for the beans of $1,600 – compared with current market prices of about $800 – and a 'social premium' of $150 per ton. I assume that this premium goes right back to the farmers, but am pleasantly surprised when it's explained to me that it goes into a trust fund to support community infrastructure. Already more than $300,000 has been accumulated and the Kuapa Kokoo Farmers' Trust takes proposals from different communities for such things as health centers, water bore holes, improvements to schools and credit schemes. There is an on-going program to sink a clean-water bore hole in each Kuapa Kokoo village that doesn't have one yet.

Kuapa's society development team also counts on a sustainable-agriculture officer to teach integrated pest management, and has a proactive program to ensure the empowerment and financial well-being of women members. The officers are quick to point out that a large number of farmers can no longer afford expensive imported pesticides, now that adjustment policies have removed price subsidies.

Cocoa is, worldwide, one of the most highly sprayed of all food crops. So going at least partially 'organic' is a practical as well as a philosophical step. The pride in the quality of the cocoa is universal, however, and of course popular with the fair-trade organizations who need '*pa pa paa*' – 'the best of the best'. The license plates of the Kuapa trucks have '*pa pa paa*' neatly inscribed on all of them.

Cocoa is like a lot of other export crops from the Majority World. In the lingo of the economists it lacks structural links, or 'spin-offs', to the domestic economy. Aside from the income accruing to individual farmers, or going into public expenditure, very little by way of job creation or industrial activity results from growing cocoa. Increasingly, producer countries are doing some of the processing before the cocoa is exported, which at least provides some extra employment.

Home-grown chocolate

In Ghana there is a small industry producing an excellent range of high-cocoa Golden Tree chocolates in the cities of Tema and Takoradi. But these are successfully kept out of the North by high tariff walls – 34 per cent in Europe – and poor economies of scale. Most of this chocolate is consumed in the very small domestic market. It is a luxury item, out of the reach of most Ghanaians. There are ambitions to build a regional market for Golden Tree, but even if these are successful markets will remain limited by low incomes and cheaper competition from the Big Chocolate of multinationals.

So it is not unreasonable for governments to tax exported cocoa as a way of spreading some of the cocoa wealth to meet the needs of the rest of society. In West Africa, the big producing countries – Ghana and Côte d'Ivoire – have done this to a point where the small cocoa farmer bears too much of the burden of state expenditure. This endangers the sustainability of the cocoa economy and now the pendulum is swinging back, to give farmers a better deal on their crop. The 'spread-effect' is more significant where cocoa remains a small-holder crop than it is on the agrochemical plantations of Indonesia, where workers make about one dollar a day.

Structural-adjustment straitjacket
While it is important for farmers to get a decent price it is also important for the governments of the South not to have their fiscal hands tied when trying to meet such basic needs as heath, education, farmer-support and infrastructure maintenance. Unfortunately, their hands are being tied by structural adjustment. In Ghana this is compounded by the problem of aging and often absentee cocoa farmers.

Another potential spin-off is the number of byproducts that can be derived from cocoa: fertilizer, animal feed and soap – as well as a range of cakes, biscuits and jams from cocoa powder. These last are being experimented with at the cocoa research station in Teme, which is also producing a gin and a brandy made from the 'sweatings' of the cocoa beans during the fermentation process. While none of these is likely to add up to much in terms of the Gross Domestic Product, they are a major part of the survival economy – the complete utilization of the crop helps sustain a way of life and the social-security system of rural Ghana.

4 Bananas in Guatemala and the Caribbean

War breaks out over the world's largest herb. Why the World Trade Organization (WTO) promotes slavery and environmental insanity. Amidst all this, what chance for the perfect, fairly traded and organic banana?

FAIR TRADE HAS to learn how to flourish in a hostile world. Convention dictates that trade must engage from time to time in skirmishes or wars. Any resemblance to an honorable duel vanishes, however, when one of the parties turns up with a machete and the other with a bazooka.

From time to time two well-matched brawlers may, nonetheless, find themselves lumbering into battle, often over a seemingly trivial matter. Such has been the case for a good while now with the United States and the European Union (EU). The matters at issue have ranged from aircraft noise to beef, but one of the noisiest spats in recent years broke out over bananas growing in the Windward Islands of the Caribbean.

Every war needs a warmonger, and in the Banana War of 1999 that role was assumed by one Carl H Lindner Jnr. He headed the American Financial Group, which included among its assets Chiquita Brands International of Cincinnati – along with the Dole Food Company and Del Monte Fresh Produce, one of the US-based Big Banana corporations that control most of the world's trade in the fruit. In mid-1999 Mr Lindner claimed he was owed $500 million on account of the European banana 'regime', and he wanted the US Government to get it back for him.

Carl H Lindner Jnr was a man of substance. His personal wealth was estimated at $830 million, much of it dredged from the murky waters of Savings and Loans institutions in the US. A strict Baptist, he had a habit of handing out little white cards with gold-embossed aphorisms on them, such as: 'I like to do my giving while I'm living so I know where it's going.' Though he preferred the Republicans and lent Robert Dole a corporate jet during the 1996 presidential campaign, when he saw the electoral tide flowing towards the Democrats he slipped Bill Clinton a quick $500,000.

A few days later the Banana War between the US Government and the EU, that had been simmering away for years, duly boiled over. If, as a result of it, Mr Lindner were to get the $500 million he reckoned he was owed, then he would have made a handsome return on his investment in Bill Clinton.

Warped world

Welcome, then, to the warped world of bananas. Or rather, to the bent business of international trade in bananas. There is a difference. For the Banana War was being waged between two regions – the US and Europe – that grow almost no bananas at all. On the other hand, the world's two largest banana producers – Brazil and India – grow them largely for domestic consumption alone and have little to do with the international trade.

Almost everywhere in the tropics the fruit of the world's largest herb has been adopted by small farmers as a prolific source of nutrition. The banana, *Musa sapiculum*, is a remarkable plant structured rather like a giant leek. There are many varieties growing in myriad settings, from a few plants for household consumption to plots for local markets. They grow fast; the stem dies back once the fruit is harvested, but already the next 'follower' is preparing to take over. Carefully tended, on the right soil, in the right climate and with minimal inputs, a plot of a couple of acres (about one hectare) can produce several bunches, with 100 to 200 bananas on each of them, every week, all year round, for 30 years.

Bananas

International trade

Less than a quarter of all the world's bananas, however, gets mixed up in international trade, and it's only when they do that they encounter the big-banana business, where things can get a bit twisted. Just one variety, Dwarf Cavendish or Gran Enano, is preferred by the world banana trade. On plantations across Central America, northern Latin America, parts of Africa and Asia, vast numbers of clones are planted out on flat land, much of which is swept by hurricanes. The deforested land on which they grow is drained and degraded. The plants are subjected to ceaseless treatment by toxic chemicals. Their unripe fruit are cut green, fragile and inedible from the stem, the bunches strung like carcasses to cableways that carry them off for scrubbing with more chemicals. Graded and packed into boxes, dispatched in refriger-ated ships ('reefers') to Europe and North America, the hapless fruit is then ripened for supermarkets and conjured into an image of 'quality' that people around the world who live in ignorance of the truth wish to consume in ever-increasing billions.

This is the 'dollar' banana that accounts for 80 per cent of the fruit we eat in the North and is controlled by Chiquita, Dole and Del Monte. They in turn are subsidiaries of conglomerates, like Mr Lindner's American Financial Group. Together, the Big Three constitute an oligopoly that controls the supply of bananas, fixes prices and has an inordinate love of secrecy. When, in May 1998, the *Cincinnati Enquirer* had the temerity to publish an exposé of how Chiquita actually operates, the company sued. It wasn't that the reports were inaccurate. Quite the reverse – they'd made use of the corporation's internal voice mail and thus violated its right to privacy. The newspaper issued an abject apology, paid Chiquita an undisclosed sum (thought to be in the region of $10 million), a journalist was sacked and prosecuted and the reports removed from its website. You bet, the Big Three mean business.

Lomé Convention

On the other side of the low-intensity Banana War was Europe and its import regime. In a Byzantine web of quotas, licenses and tariffs, the EU – the world's largest importer – was protecting the banana industries of its former colonies. These are grouped into the ACP (Africa, Caribbean, Pacific) countries to which Europe made firm commitments in the Lomé Convention of 1975, renewed four times thereafter. The Lomé agreements are by no means a passport to prosperity for the ACP countries. But banana exports are critical to a number of ACP economies, and particularly to the Windward Islands of Dominica, St Lucia, St Vincent and Grenada. Under the EU 'regime', growers here were paid roughly double the price – and incurred roughly three times the production costs – of the 'dollar' banana.

The renewed Banana War was an attempt by the Big Three, and Chiquita in particular, to get their hands on this lucrative business; to remove quota restrictions and reduce the tariffs they must pay, thereby cutting the price paid to ACP producers and putting them out of business. In 1995 the brand-new World Trade Organization (WTO) began to implement the no-less Byzantine rules that emerged from the Uruguay Round of the General Agreement on Tariffs and Trade (GATT). The WTO is empowered not merely to oversee the new rules, but to enforce them. In principle these favor trade 'liberalization', though in practice – and short of self-interest – no-one quite knows what this means. It wasn't hard, therefore, to suggest that the European banana regime conflicted with WTO rules.

However, the Banana War was not only about bananas. Much bigger fish were frying: the relative power of governments, nations, trading blocs and corporations; the structure, control and profitability of agriculture; the Common Agricultural Policy of the European Union; the fate of small-island economies; the booty of free trade.

In the form of the Banana War the WTO was given its most high-profile trial to date as the Supreme Court of Globalization. If this meant anything other than the interests of corporate oligopolies like the Big Three, then the deliberations of the WTO had yet to suggest what it was.

Meanwhile, the lives of many thousands of banana growers in the South hung in the balance. They had been there before. In fact, they had rarely been anywhere else. What did they think? How did they feel about events that affected them directly, but over which they appeared to have no influence at all?

I made a journey to find out, and I discovered something I would not otherwise have known. It became clear to me that the Banana War was being fought between two equally outdated protagonists. On the one hand, in the form of the European regime, the legacy of colonialism; on the other, in the form of the 'dollar' regime promoted by Chiquita and the US Government, plantation slavery and florid ecological insanity.

The fact that the rulings of the WTO had invariably favored the latter over the former was regrettable and potentially catastrophic in its effects. But neither of these two relics had anything useful to say about the future, which they could not, I felt sure, conceivably survive.

So the question was, what would replace them?

By this time I'd seen enough of fair trade to know it could work. It would not be unreasonable to raise my sights a little and begin to tackle a larger, recurring theme – the connection, or lack of it, between fair and 'organic' trade, between equity and the environment. Would it be possible to discover what I had come to think of as the 'perfect' banana – one that was both fairly traded and organic?

To avoid undue disappointment, I began where I was least likely to find it, in Guatemala. On its short Caribbean coastline, squashed between Honduras and Belize on a flat, swampy plain, the modern banana industry was born – and the term 'banana republic' first took on its baleful meaning.

The search begins

The ticket collector was determined to squash the mosquito. He was chasing it across the cracked wind-

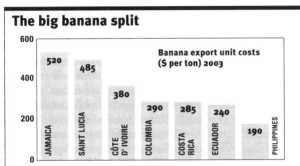

The big banana split

Banana export unit costs ($ per ton) 2003

- JAMAICA: 520
- SAINT LUCIA: 485
- CÔTE D'IVOIRE: 380
- COLOMBIA: 290
- COSTA RICA: 285
- ECUADOR: 240
- PHILIPPINES: 190

UNCTAD

The dollar banana from the plantations of the Big Three looks 'cheaper'. But the real cost of a banana is not quite what the price suggests. Over half the production costs are due to the hard labor involved. Wages in the Philippines, Ecuador or the Central American plantation economies are roughly half the incomes of small farmers in St Lucia or Jamaica. The plantations of the Big Three flourish on what is, in effect, slave labor.

The plantation system uses large quantities of chemical poisons – more than ten times the average even for intensive agriculture in industrialized countries. Nematicides – to kill nematode worms – have sterilized tens of thousands of plantation workers.

Plantations also destroy the local environment; sophisticated drainage systems leach the nutrients from the soil and, in combination with other residues like copper, leave the land sterile. The fragility of the exposed soil and the concentrated flows of water cause severe soil erosion and increased flooding during tropical storms. Large quantities of fish, coral and animal life are lost to poisonous chemical agents. ■

shield of an old American school bus as it rattled out of Puerto Barrios, the only sizable port in the region. Why did this look so odd? This was, after all, a tropical swamp, where you can usually expect to get eaten alive by mosquitoes and there's not much point in taking the trouble to kill a single one. Yet I hadn't been bitten once. And there were no birds. There was, I suddenly realized, little evidence of life of any kind.

Except, of course, for banana plants. Countless thousands of them. Mile upon endless mile, lining the roadside in numbered squares like the serried ranks of some godforsaken army decked out in uniform green headgear and ramrod trunks, holding out white plastic bags draped over growing bunches of bananas.

This was the Guatemalan territory of Chiquita Brands, a direct descendant of the United Fruit Company. They used to call this company *el pulpo* (octopus) because its tentacles reached into every crevice of Guatemalan life. Established in 1899, United Fruit pioneered the plantation system of banana cultivation and by 1949 owned 3.5 million acres (1.4 million hectares) of Jamaica, Cuba, the Dominican Republic, Panama, Honduras, Nicaragua and Colombia. Its largest domain, however, was in Guatemala, where it owned Puerto Barrios as well as every mile of railroad in the country.

In 1954 United Fruit – guided by legendary PR man Edward Bernays – orchestrated US support for the overthrow of the elected government of Jacobo Arbenz, which intended to expropriate 400,000 acres (162,000 hectares) of its land and support the demands of banana workers for better pay and conditions. Violent repression ensued and has plagued the country ever since. Anxious to distance itself from accusations that United Fruit were dictating US foreign policy, the US Government eventually began a federal antitrust suit against United Fruit's banana monopoly, and in 1958 the company was broken up.

Chiquita Brands, the Dole Food Company and Del Monte Fresh Produce, the Big Three banana companies of today, are its offspring and you can still see the resemblance in them all too clearly.

Union activist

Feliciano sat beside me on the bus. He was looking after me, though I was not entirely sure who was looking after him, an active trade unionist in a place where this is a dangerous thing to be. Gentle and attentive, he had agreed to show me something of what life is like on the banana plantations. His family had worked for bananas for 60 years: his father had 'retired' to a small-holding and absolute poverty some time previously, but he and all his brothers still worked on the plantations.

The bus slowed to a halt. A man in a sap-blotched vest, seated on what looked like a broomstick, hurtled out of the banana plants to one side of us, floated across the road in front and disappeared into the plants on the other side. The ticket collector, who had killed the mosquito, got off the bus and pushed back an overhead rail so that we could proceed. In due course we caught up with the man on the broomstick, punting rhythmically through the banana plants with two poles, flying along the cable-way that was made to carry off their fruit, into spotlights of burning sunlight, like Tinkerbell across a stage set for Peter Pan.

'Stop the bus! We're getting off!' cried Feliciano, some distance further on.

We stood in the dust left by the departing bus, in front of a large, dark barn of corrugated iron. Inside were empty concrete tanks, benches of steel rollers, industrial remains with mysterious functions. Octaviano and Guillermo watched us guardedly as we approached.

'Welcome to Alabama/Arizona,' said Feliciano. 'The *finca* [literally 'farm', but better translated here as 'plantation'] that belongs to Victor Manuel Morales Hausseler. In theory, at least. *Compañeros* Octaviano and Guillermo will explain.'

Meeting the workers

'We are totally destitute,' said Octaviano. 'Totally destitute. We have nothing to eat or drink. They cut off the electricity and the water. We have to drink polluted water from wells. We're being poisoned.'

From the tremor in his voice I sensed the force of frustration in a story told too often and to no effect. 'Well, we're just sitting here. Waiting. There used to be more than two hundred of us, men, women and children. But some have drifted away. There are about a hundred of us left. Like I said, we're just waiting.'

'For what?' I asked.

'For something to happen,' said Octaviano.

'It began with the women,' interrupted Guillermo, suddenly animated. 'The way they were treated. They were the ones working here in the packing plant. They had to use chemicals that made them sick, in the washing tanks, gave them sores on their feet. All times of the day, and late into the night too. Many of them are single mothers, and they weren't allowed to feed their children. Well, it got to the point where we weren't prepared to put up with it any more.'

'The only way to protect ourselves was with a union,' said Octaviano. 'There were lots of rumors flying around. The company was getting jumpy. Part of the plantation is on the other side of the river, and there's a bridge across it for the cableway, which we had to use to get to work. They came with armed guards and dogs to stop us crossing it, to split us up. So we were forced to use small boats. The river is very dangerous. Sometimes the guards would shoot into the water, trying to scare us. And then we were all sacked, with almost a week's wages still owing to us. The company has broken the labor laws of this country. The Government should be enforcing the law, but it doesn't. The courts are always on the side of the companies. We've been waiting to be reinstated ever since.'

'When did this happen?' I asked.

'February,' said Guillermo.

'Six months ago?' I asked with alarm.

'Eighteen months ago,' said Octaviano.

A few months after I left I heard that the Government had finally been persuaded to promote a settlement that recognized the union and reinstated at least some of the workers in their jobs – a small, if fragile victory achieved against apparently hopeless odds.

A few miles further down the road we entered a village where a thousand people lived – the families of the workers on Finca la Inca, at the end of the bus route and almost into Honduras. Stunted trees and mean little hutches lined the only street. As Feliciano and I strolled through the village we were followed by a man in uniform carrying a pump-action shotgun. Crawling behind him was a Pepsi delivery truck. It used to be raided by children under contract to Pepsi bootleggers. In Guatemala, value is signified by the size of the weapons touted around it.

We first saw Francisco sitting outside his house. He was on the executive of the Finca la Inca union, which was recognized by the company. Reluctantly and slowly, the Big Three had been accepting trade unions on some of the *fincas* they controlled. Feliciano believed that by improving international links between banana unions in the early 1990s the *Co-ordinadora de Sindicatos Bananeros de América Latina* (banana unions' federation), based in Costa Rica and Honduras, had had a marked impact. Guatemalan labor law only permits the formation of unions in individual companies. So there were many small unions, one for every *finca* of 200-or-so workers, and communication between them was difficult.

Bananas

Francisco, Feliciano and I sat down. There were only two chairs, so Francisco squeezed himself into his child's chair which cracked ominously under his weight. We were joined by Ubaldo, a powerfully built man just in from an eight-hour shift on the plantation. He was plainly exhausted, sinking into a tiny hammock strung between two trees. We talked about the difficulties they faced.

Wage freeze

Their wages averaged $0.63 an hour, $28 a week. Fixed almost three years previously, the rate was overdue for review. But the companies had made full use of Hurricane Mitch, the terrible storm that hung over the region for four days in October 1998. Though the devastation and death toll in Guatemala did not reach the same levels as in neighboring Honduras, still the rivers here had ripped away bridges and filled houses with silt, flooding banana plantations along their banks. The companies extended the wage agreement and sacked 'redundant' union members, claiming the damage done by Mitch as the reason.

At COBSA (a Guatemalan front company for Dole) they went one stage further. Members of the 'yellow' company union were induced to make legal complaints against the independent trade union, claiming its members were responsible for 'damages and prejudice' valued at $7.5 million in the wake of Mitch. Armed guards with dogs stripped the roofs off their houses to force them to leave the *finca*. The courts duly issued *ordenes de captura* (arrest warrants) against 150 union members. Most were still in hiding, though among those arrested was a union official in Guatemala City. It said little for the case against him – or any of the others – that his passport proved he had been in Britain attending an international conference on poverty at the time the 'damage' was alleged to have been done in Guatemala.

Chemical cocktail

Along the roads were posted 'Notices to the Public' warning against entering the plantations while aerial fumigation was underway. The Big Three claim that they do not fumigate when workers are in their plantations. Feliciano, Francisco and Ubaldo laughed at the claim. If the workers got out every time fumigation took place there'd have been no bananas cut at all.

Free trade unions – a dark hard history

UN-sponsored Peace Accords were drawn up in Guatemala in 1997, formally bringing to an end 40 years of genocidal conflict which left hundreds of thousands dead and 45,000 'disappeared'. People expressed relief that the Accords had been agreed. But the underlying conflicts remained largely unresolved, and among these was the relentless persecution of the Guatemalan labor movement.

UNSITRAGUA, based in Guatemala City, represented some 74 member unions active across a wide range of employment, from the maquila export-processing factories to rural workers and banana plantations. It still had to operate semi-clandestinely, despite the Accords which gave assurances on free trade unions, and UNSITRAGUA activists continued to feature on blacklists for arrest and assassination.

'We have a dark, hard history,' said Julio Coj of UNSITRAGUA. 'You could not speak or say what you felt and suffered, because you would be assassinated immediately. But we think that if we keep hiding our faces and our names, then we endorse the impunity that the Government and business sector still try to maintain.'

That much, he said, remained unchanged. 'We have peace on paper, but not a real and concrete peace. To make that we need full respect for union rights and for collective bargaining. The Government does not play its proper role, which is to balance business and union interests. There needs to be a radical change of attitude in business mentality and especially in the courts, which should uphold such meager protection as we get from our labor laws, in conformity with the conventions of the International Labor Organization. But they remain in the pocket of big business.'

'What matters for the workers is that the Government makes sure that all transnational companies respect the law. At the moment that's getting much more difficult, because globalization is allowing transnationals to produce what they like where they like, with no impediments. The tragedy is that this process is creating more, not less, poverty for us in Latin America.' ■

'It's not so bad in the mornings,' said Ubaldo. 'But, as the heat increases, these foul-smelling chemicals seem to rise up in the air, you have to inhale them and you begin to feel nauseous and have difficulty breathing.'

I asked what the chemicals were called. They had no idea. Francisco fetched a wad of blue plastic strips. These are sometimes placed around the stems of the bunches as a substitute for the intensely toxic concentrations in the plastic bags used to protect the growing fruit. He asked me to smell them. There was a deep foulness to the odor.

Feliciano had given me a copy of the *pacto collectivo*, the union agreement they had fought long and hard to achieve at the Pamaxan plantation, where he worked. On the face of it, this was a benign document granting the union formal recognition. But there were clauses regulating almost every aspect of their daily lives; not just working conditions and pay but schools, healthcare, water and electricity supplies, housing, transport, recreation facilities, books for the union library, football shirts, basketballs, toys for the children, even clocks.

At Finca la Inca I looked around me and asked if there was anything, besides the union, that wasn't controlled by the company.

'No,' said Francisco. 'Not apart from the Catholic Church over there.' He pointed to a wooden shed across the street. 'And the company refused to give them electricity. So they have to pray in the dark.'

Did he ever eat bananas?

'Good lord, no!' he said, looking genuinely surprised. 'People in places like this don't eat the fruit of their labor.'

I reflected to myself that although the offspring of the 'octopus' that was United Fruit had had, by 1999, precisely 100 years to establish their value to the local community, they had achieved nothing. From time to time they acted as if they didn't want to poison their employees or pay them shameful wages. But they were hooked. Always they had pulled back, resorted to crude coercion, because otherwise they were at risk of extinction. In truth, despite the outward appearance of a modern, efficient agricultural industry, they were an industrial dinosaur.

All the talk of *ordenes de captura* and guns and dogs and escape into hiding brought a single word to my mind, but I had refrained from using it because of the sensitivities involved. Ubaldo's great form, exhausted but relaxed now, swung in the tiny hammock. He looked into the distance in silence.

'It's just this wretched poverty,' he said eventually. 'We cannot get away from it. You know what it is?'

'You tell me,' I said.

'Slavery,' he said.

Exactly the word I'd had in mind.

Next stop: Dominica

I had taken a big step away from the perfect banana. So I flew off to the Windward Islands, across the Caribbean from Guatemala, to see if something closer to it could be found on the other side of the Banana War front line. I'd picked on the island of Dominica.

'We don't want to be in a market competing with producers like Chiquita,' said Gregory Shillingford emphatically, 'with a fruit that doesn't taste good, uses a lot of chemicals and employs slave labor. We do not want to endanger our environment. We want to promote reasonable wages for all working people, and a good relationship with consumers.'

Well, this made something of a change, and if any one person in Dominica could make this happen then I guess it had to be Gregory Shillingford. As General Manager of the Dominica Banana Marketing Corporation (DBMC) he was a key figure in the island's banana trade and carried a big responsibility on his broad shoulders. Dominicans rely very heavily on bananas, which account for some 20 per cent of Gross Domestic Product, 60 per cent of exports of goods, and the income of maybe 10,000 people – a very large chunk of the 90,000 population.

But bananas had also delivered this tiny island's people into a fatal reliance on a single export crop that had also, inevitably, betrayed them. Production was in headlong decline. In the peak year of 1988, 72,000 tons of bananas were exported from 15,000 acres (6,075 hectares) of cultivation by 7,000 growers. But then falling prices, a spate of hurricanes, a tangled and more 'liberalized' single market in the EU after 1992, all took their toll. In 1998 just 28,000 tons had been exported from 7,000 acres (2,835 hectares) by 2,800 growers – a reduction by more than a half. In villages around the island, stores that once sold basic necessities, most of them imported with banana money, had closed down.

Even so, preferential access to the EU market continued. Between them, the Windward Islands still had an annual, duty-free quota of some 287,000 tons of bananas. Yet they sometimes used less than a half of it. Growers were evidently either unwilling or unable to produce more bananas. They were deserting the battlefront. If the European banana regime was such a good deal, why should this have been so?

Shillingford quoted a telling statistic: more than 80 per cent of the total crop in Dominica came from just 1,200 growers. The remaining 1,600 relied on the DBMC's obligation to buy their bananas. 'We don't really mind,' he said, a little halfheartedly. 'But what we need is growers who are business people, not peasants.'

Growers' gripes
Small farmers who own their own land are not, however, merely a quaint feature of Dominican society. They have shaped its history almost entirely, giving it

an idiosyncratic, egalitarian, periodically febrile nature. No-one with any sense, like Gregory Shillingford, assumes that their interests can be taken lightly.

'Lots of small growers, particularly the older ones, are giving up their banana plots because it's all getting far too difficult, far too regimented,' said Irvince Auguiste as we pass a bedraggled collection of abandoned plants on a steep hillside. For ten years Irvince was the elected Chief – 'rather like being Mayor' he said – of the Carib Territory, through which we were driving. In 1902 some 3,000 acres (1,215 hectares) on the east coast of the island were handed back by the British to the few remaining descendants of the indigenous Carib peoples. Today, 3,700 of their heirs hold the same land in common, from which some 200 growers still produce bananas. They are a reminder that this is a rather special place.

'It used to be a much simpler thing,' continued Irvince. 'People would grow bananas and do other things as well. Now you have to keep diaries and charts and add up columns of figures and do exactly what you're told if you want to be a certified grower and get a decent price for your bananas. There's no time for anything else.

'Then you've got to be able to bounce back from hurricanes, which keep destroying your crop. Remember, small farmers have very little security. They can never be quite sure how good their crop will be, or when the next hurricane will strike, or even if there'll be a crop at all. It's not like having a regular wage and it's very easy to get into debt, because you have to invest in the crop before it is harvested. Sometimes they abandon bananas and then, when they find they can't earn a living from anything else, go back to them again. My father grew bananas, and I carried them on my head as a boy. But I don't grow them myself. Just recently, though, I've been having second thoughts...'

Bananas

A big, red, battered pickup hurtled towards us round a hairpin bend. Irvince signaled to the driver, scarcely visible above the steering wheel, who screeched to a halt and wound down the window. She was slightly breathless. They chatted.

'Balene Fredrick,' said Irvince as she took off again. 'Just having a breather from the softball cricket match, to check on her kids. You know, she's one of our best banana growers. Let's go back and talk to her.' We set off in pursuit. She'd already disappeared round the next bend. 'What a woman!' sighed Irvince, awestruck.

More means less

Balene and three of her kids were waiting for us in a roadside tin shed. Every small grower had a 'field' packing shed like hers. Handsome bunches of freshly cut bananas were laid out on tiered shelves, graded by size and labeled 'Geest'. In front of the bench was a large plastic bowl containing a washing solution. Chemicals were used here too, but much more sparingly than in Guatemala. Pinned to the back of the shed were complicated charts showing how the color-coded production cycle had to be followed. You could tell how she cared for her bananas from the way she handled them.

I asked her how much she earned from them each week. 'Just about enough to keep the children,' she said. 'What with their clothes and food and schooling, they cost a lot of money. In a way, I wish I didn't have to grow bananas. It never stops, and you have to do everything just right. It seems to get harder and harder, and we seem to earn less and less.'

There were few alternatives. The island was one of the most beautiful places I had ever seen. But it attracted few tourists. There was no airport for wide-bodied jets, and therefore no golf courses, casinos or 'resort' hotels. White sandy beaches and blue lagoons were few and far between. Tentative steps were being taken towards eco-tourism, to complement Dominica's chosen image as 'The Nature Island'. A 'rainforest tramway' was being constructed 'for the less-athletic eco-tourist'.

There were firm plans, too, for an international airport. This would have destroyed homes, a school and scarce acres of relatively flat, productive agricultural land. It would have plunged the people of Dominica deeply into debt, as well as the quagmire of graft that surrounds all such projects. Short of selling their land to hotels and golf courses, changing into flunky clothes and training to be servile, it was hard to see how mass tourism would benefit most Dominicans – or suit their disposition.

One possibility that had indeed been discussed, said Gregory Shillingford, was organic and fairly traded bananas. Some 15,000 acres (6,075 hectares) of banana land had lain fallow for at least five years (and were therefore free of chemicals), and the growers owned their own land, so the potential was there. So far, however, no-one had taken the plunge. Perhaps there was another future for this extraordinary place that had yet to be disentangled from its history.

Indeed, some time after I left, headway was made and the Windward Islands began to develop fairly traded and organic exports. The need for this became increasingly urgent as banana prices collapsed. This simultaneously increased the interest in fair trade among desperate banana growers – and made the price of fair-trade bananas for consumers in the North seem that much higher by comparison. Fair trade in bananas faced its next severe test.

Dominican Republic
However, while I may have got closer to the perfect banana in Dominica than in Guatemala, I had not yet found it and still did not even know whether it even

existed. I set off for the Dominican Republic, my final destination, with few expectations. The country is little more prosperous than Guatemala, and considerably less so than Dominica. Like Guatemala, it has suffered from the attentions of the United States, including an invasion by US marines. Bordered to the west by Haiti (one of the most poverty-stricken countries in the world) the Dominican Republic already is what Dominica threatens to become – a center for mass tourism. So I traveled to Ázua, close to the border with Haiti – and far from the cosmetics of tourism around the capital, Santo Domingo – feeling that my quest was probably futile.

And then I ran into an extraordinary story. It really began in 1992, with a small environmental disaster. In the mountains that march westwards across the troubled border with Haiti, there were 250 families living in a state of virtual destitution. They began to burn down the forest in which they lived, to make charcoal for sale.

'We didn't really want to do it,' said Angel Custodio, a shrewd, articulate man who was in the early years of an active retirement. 'The forest is a living thing, and we were killing it. We knew it couldn't last long. Our environment is alive, and we want to protect it. But we had no choice, no other way of making a living. So we asked the Government for help.'

They got lucky. The Government built an entire village for Angel's community, complete with utilities, paved roads, health center, school, church and halfway decent houses, on the coastal plain just outside the small town of Ázua. It also handed over to them a plot of fallow, fertile land large enough for every family to have its own 'parcel' of at least two hectares – sufficient to live from. So the erstwhile charcoal burners set to work growing maize, yucca, ground provisions – and a few bananas. They used no chemicals because, admitted Angel Custodio, they simply didn't have the money. The people of Finca 6 would doubtless have remained in much the same situation had it not been for two further strokes of good fortune. Well, the first must have been a mixed blessing. I have never been anywhere quite so hot. Even inside the cab of an air-conditioned pickup the thermometer registered well over 40 degrees centigrade. The heat is, however, relatively dry. That is bad news for plant diseases that need a good dose of humidity to flourish. But, with a high water table beneath them and good irrigation, it is very good news indeed for bananas.

Their second piece of good fortune was that, around the towns of Monte Cristi and Mao in the north of the country, two Dutch agencies were helping to develop fairer ways of producing bananas. Solidaridad and Max Havelaar (pioneers in the fair-trade coffee business) were making some headway across notoriously stony ground.

Savid to the rescue

So too was a young Dutch woman, Jetta van den Berg. In 1994 she set up a marketing company in Ázua she named Savid SA – an elision of *salud* ('health') and *vida* ('life'). Savid took on the tricky business of developing an unconventional product: organic bananas. It worked. The company helped to make the Dominican Republic the world's largest producer of organic bananas, with over 80 per cent of the total. Though accounting for just 27,000 tons in 1998, the world market for organic bananas was expanding fast, at an average 30 per cent per year, and demand consistently exceeded supply.

So Savid had to go looking for more producers and approached Finca 6. 'The market for organic bananas looked as if it was better than for our other produce,' said Angel, 'and so we began to develop our production for Savid. And now we do think, one hundred per cent, that organic production is better than conventional methods. I assure you, we're not just thinking about our own lives, our own health, but the lives and health of consumers as well, and about how to develop our own country – and why not others as well?'

Fresh approach

A severe test came in September 1998, when Hurricane George swept across the Dominican Republic and destroyed most of the country's banana crop, including that of Finca 6. In marked contrast with the way the Big Three exploited Mitch in Guatemala, Savid continued to finance the growers through to recovery, and they were now returning to full production, their confidence shaken but intact.

Porfirio Acosta Gil had a mobile phone that never stopped ringing. 'One request after another!' he sighed. 'I should turn the damn thing off.' He was the Production Manager for Savid, the head of a team of agronomists and evidently a revered figure.

All around us were flourishing banana plants that lived without chemicals of any kind. Porfirio assured me that it was real enough. Organic certification was by the German agency BCS, and tests were rigorous.

There was nothing very mysterious about it, he explained. The prime requirement was for meticulous tending of the plants, cutting away dying leaves, keeping the topsoil clean, removing the flowers from the bunches at the right time, covering them with reusable, chemical-free plastic bags to encourage growth and prevent damage from birds and surrounding leaves.

The same 'one follower' system was used here as elsewhere: successive shoots were named 'mother', 'daughter', 'granddaughter' and others were prevented from growing. Because of the aridity, the lower stem of the 'mother' was preserved after cutting, to allow its moisture to drain into the successor shoots. There were irrigation channels that used ground water pumped from wells. Spraying was with citrus oil which controlled most, if not all, banana diseases. Organic fertilizer was imported from Costa Rica, though production was being developed locally. We visited the plant, where large piles of animal droppings and compost attracted the most gigantic mosquitoes, and I was bitten at last.

Porfirio had the air of someone who knew his talents. I imagined that his skills could have commanded very much bigger rewards from straightforward commercial companies.

'You know, for all the bother of this job, I get tremendous satisfaction from it,' he said. 'It satisfies me, it really does, to be involved in something that people are committed to, with people who are overcoming their poverty, with building something good. At this moment, I wouldn't want to do anything else.'

Associated benefits

At first, the individual farmers of Finca 6 weren't so sure how to work together. Jetta van den Berg and Savid were insistent that they should make up their minds: dealing with each one of them individually would be impossible. 'We thought about forming a co-operative,' said Angel. 'But, well, our experience of rural co-operatives hasn't always been very positive. Too much cheating, I'm afraid. So we decided to set up an Association. Each of us still owns our "parcel", but we all belong to the Association, which meets regularly, elects officers to deal with Savid and things that affect us all. For example, if one *parcelero* doesn't tend the plants properly there's a risk of disease spreading to all of us.'

Angel took some satisfaction from the fact that neighboring growers now wanted to join Finca 6. That, he believed, was a real measure of its success. The best advice he could give them was to form their own association, and Finca 6 would help them. 'We want people, especially poor people, to be united.

Bananas

If you have money, then you can live as you like. But if, like us, you don't, then sometimes you're going to need a service from somebody that isn't money, a service given individually, personally, between people. By being organized we can achieve this.'

And so, in 1997, Finca 6 was certified as a fair-trade producer by Max Havelaar. As we talked we sat beneath the roof of a new *comedor* (diner and meeting place) for the growers – one product of the fair-trade price premium they received. There were plans to build much-needed warehousing as well.

Finca 6 had achieved something very, very rare: an organic and fairly traded product. I tried thinking of this extraordinary achievement as mere good fortune, unrepeatable elsewhere. But is it just a matter of luck that a government justifies its existence from time to time, and assists the people it claims to represent? Was it mere coincidence that, in the face of such a dreadful trade, people everywhere should have defied bleak orthodoxy and searched for something better? Of course not.

Fairly traded and organic

Fair trade can still apply, even where organic production is not possible. Organic production can still take place, even where fair trade hasn't yet been achieved. Between them they could account for a much larger share of the banana business than they currently do. But it is only when they come together that organic production ceases to reflect the narrow self-interest of consumers, and fair trade fully respects the environment. Each complements the other.

Still, I had to have my doubts about Finca 6, if only because I knew what they were up against, and how far they still had to travel. For a start, the members of Finca 6 had turned over their plots almost completely to the production of bananas, creating dependency on a single export crop at the expense of their own food.

Quite apart from hurricanes, the risks they faced were daunting. Organic methods were still not completely effective against some of the most virulent banana ailments, such as Black Saratoga and fungus. Then again, and sooner or later, the international market for organic bananas would surely prove as treacherous as any other. Savid SA itself had just one shareholder: Jetta van den Berg. A great deal seemed to depend on her.

Working together

I walked with Porfirio through the *parcel* of Heriberto Custodio, who was the current President of the Association. My doubts began to fade into perspective. Just as I had been told they would, other *parceleros* arrived to give Heriberto a hand. They worked with their machetes in an easy rhythm, cutting back surplus shoots, cleaning the irrigation channels, lopping off unhealthy leaves, chatting and joking as they went.

They did not have the driven, mechanical movements of rural laborers, though the work was no less strenuous in the tremendous heat. Porfirio looked around with sharp eyes, pointing from time to time to a leaf here that needed pruning, a flower there that needed plucking, the first evidence of leaf spot; coaxing, teaching, encouraging.

'These plants are so productive,' he said. 'You know, they are just as productive as on the big plantations. Perhaps more so. All it takes is a little knowledge, care and skill. And a lot of hard work, of course.'

I asked him how much a *parcelero* could earn.

'I don't really know, and I don't ask. But I've been told it's about $1,000 a month, and can be as much as $2,000.'

We were invited to Heriberto's house. In the dining room a meal of fresh vegetables, rice and chicken was laid out for us. Heriberto gently complained about the unpaid labor he had to put in at the Association, the constant disputes he must resolve, the importance of what he had to do. But the trace of a smile never quite left his lips.

'You must be very proud of what you have achieved,' I said.

'Oh yes we are,' cut in Heriberto's wife. 'You should have seen how we lived in the mountains, what this place was like when we first arrived. Now we can live with dignity. Here there is a future for our children.'

And then she brought in the bananas.

'You eat bananas?' I said

'Of course!' said Heriberto. 'They are very good for you, you know. Very nourishing. Very tasty. Don't you think it would be a little strange if we didn't eat them?'

Fair-trade and organic bananas

The criteria for organic products are now firmly established and scientifically verifiable. For fair trade the situation is more complex. But, as for other fair-trade products, they include direct links between consumers and producers, a guaranteed minimum price and a price premium for producers, favorable financing and long-term commitments.

In 1997 bananas represented only a tiny part of an organic market that was estimated to be worth $10 billion worldwide. The European Union was the world's largest organic market, and Germany the largest consumer of organic bananas, with sales of over 6,000 tons in 1998. Britain was next, at about half that level. The US imported a similar quantity to Germany, and supplied the Canadian market.

The Dominican Republic was by far the largest producer, followed by Mexico. Japan imported 2,700 tons of organic bananas in 1997, mainly from the Philippines but also from Australia. Prospects for the market were thought to be extremely good, the main constraint being difficulties with supply. The price premium at retail level varied from 50 to 200 per cent. Europe was also the largest market for fair-trade goods and in 1996 established the Fair Trade Labeling Organization International (FLO), an NGO which holds the register of certified producers across a growing range of products. The leading importer of fair-trade bananas was Agrofair, a joint venture formed by the Dutch NGO Solidaridad and producers in developing countries. Agrofair pioneered fair-trade bananas on the Dutch market and accounted for more than 60 per cent of fair-trade banana imports into Europe. Their launch in the Netherlands in 1996 brought a market share of ten per cent within a few months and averaged five per cent – the highest

'Very strange indeed,' I agreed.

I peeled back the skin, placed the naked fruit on my plate, cut a delicate slice, speared it with a fork and slipped it into my mouth.

'Well, what do you think?' asked Heriberto's wife.

'Delicious!' I said.

'Organic and fairly traded,' said Porfirio.

'Perfect,' I said.

---

share for any fair-trade product in the country. The share in Switzerland remained at ten per cent. The price premium at retail level averaged 20 per cent. Total imports into Western Europe rose from 12,500 tons in 1997 to 17,366 tons in 1998.

The main suppliers were farmers' co-operatives in Ecuador, the Dominican Republic and Costa Rica, as well as a farm in Ghana.

AlterTrade Japan had been importing fair-trade bananas from Negros in the Philippines since 1989. In Canada the Sustainable Development Institute and Oxfam Canada were looking to introduce the product into British Colombia under the Fair Fruit Initiative. Early in 2000, fair-trade bananas were launched in several supermarkets in Britain, and the initial results were extremely encouraging.

Surveys suggest that 7.5 per cent of European consumers would buy fair-trade bananas at a price premium of ten per cent, which translates into 300,000 tons a year. The need to buy import licenses as 'newcomers' under the European banana regime was the biggest constraint – in 1999 the allocation was limited to 276 tons per 'newcomer'. Large premiums therefore had to be paid to buy licenses from other holders, inflating the retail price to consumers and reducing payments to producers.

Thanks to concerted action by consumers and an international alliance of trade unions, farmers' associations and non-governmental organizations, bananas carrying a 'fairtrade' guarantee on the label were also available in supermarkets in 13 European countries by April 2002. Six years after their launch, over 30,000 tonnes of bananas were produced and sold under fairer terms of trade: a twelve-fold increase. By 2001 Fair-trade labeled bananas made up more than 20 per cent of the Swiss banana market. ■

5 Blue jeans

Would heaven have descended to earth if cars and computers were fairly traded too? A moment to consider whether the principles of fair trade can be made to apply more widely.

FAIR TRADE DOES work, at least for producers of tropical commodities like coffee, cocoa and bananas that cannot be grown in the North. The trouble is that unfair trade does not stop here. By far the largest part of international trade, in terms of money value at least, takes place not in commodities but in manufactured goods – the things that raw commodities are eventually made into. What about fair trade in computers, motorcars, garments?

The majority of the world's manufacturing labor force now works in the countries of the South, rather than in the rich North. Improved transport and communications have made it possible to manufacture things almost anywhere in the world. The South's 'comparative advantage' is in cheap labor, so it makes sense, on the face of it, to locate labor-intensive activity there. Export-processing factories have proliferated, and with them one of the defining features of globalization. Few motorcars, for example, are now made in any one country: the thousands of parts in the average family car come from literally dozens of different countries. Economic orthodoxy suggests that in this way wealth is rapidly reaching around the world as free trade spreads its wings.

There are, as you might imagine, flaws in this interpretation. The first is that free trade doesn't actually exist. There remain massive tariffs raised against those imports from the South that compete directly with 'value added' activities in the North. For example, a tariff of 34 per cent is levied against processed chocolate (as opposed to cocoa beans) imported into the European Union from countries like Ghana. Similar tariffs and quotas were raised against textiles produced in the South, under what was known as the Multifiber Arrangement (MFA) that survived in the new rules of the World Trade Organization (WTO) for 10 years. The MFA was particularly significant because textiles, which are labor-intensive to produce, have traditionally been the 'first rung on the ladder' towards industrial prosperity – most recently in places like Hong Kong and the other 'export-led' economies of Southeast Asia. When the ten years expired in 2005, however, and the MFA lapsed, an immediate 'crisis' resulted in millions of garments from China being impounded by the EU.

The advocates of 'trade not aid' point out, with some justification, that the South loses far more from the tariffs imposed in the North than it gains from aid. Truly free trade would therefore benefit the South. What makes this argument difficult to dispute is that the tariffs are purportedly imposed to save jobs in the North, and so are frequently advocated by trade unions, fearing a wages 'race to the bottom'. The mere threat of 'relocation' to a cheap-labor country like China exerts a very real downward pressure on wage levels in the North – which is one reason why they have stagnated or fallen, and the rich-poor divide has grown even in rich countries.

Radical approach

Though calling for tariffs to save 'runaway' jobs in the North may seem like the only practicable alternative, in the longer term a much more radical approach towards working conditions is required. This hinges on the ability of the international labor movement to organize around basic standards, such as those set out by the International Labor Organization (ILO), which the majority of the world's governments have endorsed. This way, the movement has a common

The family saloon car

A typical mass-produced small family saloon sold in, say, Denmark, will have been made in literally dozens of different countries, perhaps something like this:

BELGIUM
Tubes, seat pads, brakes, radio

CANADA
Glass, radio

NETHERLANDS
Tires, paints, final assembly

SWEDEN
Hose clamps, cylinder bolt, down pipes

SWITZERLAND
Underbody coating, speedometer

UNITED STATES
Valves, hydraulic tappet

MEXICO
Wheel nuts, lamps, steering wheel

SOUTH AFRICA
Clutch case, suspension brushes

MAURITIUS
Windscreen washer pump

INDIA
Carburettor, suspension brushes, steering shaft and joint

ITALY
Cylinder head, defroster grill

AUSTRIA
Radiator and heater hoses

DENMARK
Fan belt

NORWAY
Exhaust flanges

FRANCE
Alternator, master cylinder, clutch release bearings

INDONESIA
Seat stitching, hose clamps, switches, weatherstrips

JAPAN
Starter motor, alternator, cone and roller bearings, windscreen washer pump

SPAIN
Air filter, mirrors

BRAZIL
Oil pump, distributor, body panels

BRITAIN
Rocker arm, clutch, distributor, flywheel ring gear, heater, fuel tank, steering wheel

GERMANY
Locks, pistons, front disc, cylinder head gasket, battery

World Bank.

project: the other way, national movements are at each others' throats.

Transnational corporations control a much greater proportion of world trade (about two-thirds) than they do of more local 'domestic' trade. The growth of world trade strengthens their hand immeasurably. For this reason, if for no other, they have a vested interest in promoting it regardless of the consequences. The fact that the average breakfast, say, will have traveled some 5,000 miles (8,000 kilometers) to reach stomachs in the North, rather than jogged in from local food markets, is therefore a cause for celebration. If this means that hungry countries export food, so much the better. What would otherwise be patently insane suddenly seems to make sense.

So far, it is only fair-traders who have engaged in the detail of practical alternatives. The fact that they have been able to show what can be done, even in such a 'niche market' as Southern food commodities, naturally stimulates curiosity as to how the same principles might be applied more generally. What happens if we take a similar interest in something as iconic as, say, a pair of blue jeans?

Blue jeans
My love affair with blue jeans began when I got into a bath with my very first pair. In the days before pre-shrunk denim, this was what I thought you had to do with jeans labeled 'shrink-to-fit' – a fine early example of marketing spin.

There was about them a special aura. Hard to find in the shops, they could be repaired, embroidered, 'personalized'. You could stitch things on to them or cut them off. They were adaptable, from drainpipes to flares. You could make a statement without saying a word. They made you distinctive yet free from the fear of looking odd. In fact, in blue jeans you could be whatever you wanted: masculine, feminine, granny, groupie, peasant, potentate. Whoever you were, you could be someone else.

The original associations came, of course, from America via the Wild West and the Hollywood dream factory – youthful, individualistic, forward-looking. They were hard to resist if you were growing up as I was, in a war-weary, unctuous Britain still gazing backwards into the imperial sunset.

Icon status

Jeans went on to become an icon that clothed the universal promise of postwar consumer capitalism, insinuating the American Dream into the aspirations of anyone who could be persuaded to share it. Today you can find them down gold mines in South Africa, up mountains in the Peruvian Andes, from the forests of the Congo to the catwalks of New York and Paris. When the flamboyant young designer of Paris haute couture, John Galliano, was asked on TV what he thought was the single most important garment of all time, you just knew he had to say 'jeans'.

I'm not sure when all this began to wear thin. Perhaps it was when sick 'poverty chic' and 'grunge' hit the fashion catwalks in the 1990s, followed by 'heroin chic' in New York, both clad in blue denim. Or maybe 'youth' figured out that if you aspire to be someone else for too long you become nobody at all and end up in uniform. And then, since all jeans are basically the same, paying double for the new breed of 'designer' labels is hardly so smart.

In any event, after a boom in the 1980s sparked by the global selling-fest of the Los Angeles Olympics, sales of blue jeans and the labeled footwear that went with them began to slow and then fall away.

One day a young woman from Guatemala came to see me. She described to me her daily life in a (South) Korean-owned *maquila* – export factory – stitching jackets for the American market. Driven on by shrieking supervisors, she said, she made so many jackets in a day, and for so little money, that I could scarcely believe her. She assured me this was better than having no job at all. As she talked, so softly, she trembled almost imperceptibly. News had already reached home that she had been speaking out. There had been threats against her children. I must not print her name or take her photograph. All that remained with me were her words.

So I remembered what I should never have allowed myself to forget. The true nature of a thing is not to be found in its 'image'. It lies in the materials and the people who made it. The icons of consumer capitalism are made in secret: the raw materials plundered from behind the perimeter fences of private property; the 'goods' stitched together in 'postmodern' labor camps, anonymous sheds filled with human misery, scattered around the world along the meandering borderline between consumers and producers, profit and loss. The 'image' of consumer capitalism lies.

Cotton facts

Jeans are made from cotton, and cotton has spread across five per cent of the earth's cultivable surface, invading fertile land in hungry communities, sucking them dry with irrigation, shrouding them in poison. Cotton uses higher volumes of more toxic pesticides than any other crop. A quarter of the world's pesticides are sprayed on it, causing a million cases of human poisoning every year. More than half the cotton growing in the US in genetically modified. To make the fabric, cotton is treated with another concoction of chemicals. The dyes are made from synthetic toxins. Most of the vast quantities of toxins released by the textiles industry into the air, soil and water derive from the dyeing process. Fragile parts of New Mexico have been destroyed by the extraction of pumice for 'stone washing' jeans.

Blue jeans

Fabric is too floppy, the human body too irregular and the stitching too intricate to allow for much automation beyond the sewing machine and the individual operator – almost always a young woman – making one garment at a time. This is very laborious. So jeans are stitched together in hundreds upon thousands of 'sweatshops' that have sniffed out the lowest wages in the world in places like Guatemala, Bangladesh and the Philippines, or in the immigrant 'rag trade' areas of Los Angeles, New York, Toronto, Sydney and London.

As a stock item, jeans have fallen prey to the concentration of capital in the retail sector – that is, to an ever-smaller number of ever-larger retail chains that sell most of the garments we wear. They dictate what gets made, and collect half the retail price of the garment for their pains. It is their business to promote the slightest modification in design as a significant shift in fashion – and a good reason to buy yet another pair of jeans.

So now, in the 'postmodern' age, our largest and most useful industry, supplying a necessity little less basic than food, has headed off in a cloud of poison back to the dark, satanic mills of the 19th century. This we call 'development'.

The benefit of all this is said to be that consumer capitalism provides us with endless convenience and choice. From the $10 working pair of blue jeans to the upscale designer 'label' selling for $100 and more, there's a pair for everyone.

But suppose you want something quite elementary – a garment that isn't drenched in poison and sweat. With a straightforward commodity, like coffee, you can quite readily find fairly-traded brands. But applying similar principles of environmental sanity and social justice to the complexities of cotton cultivation, spinning, dyeing, weaving, cutting, stitching, the rag trade and the fashion business in general is quite another matter.

The first step on the ladder

The Newly Industrializing Countries (NICs) or 'Little Tigers' of Southeast Asia began by exporting textiles and clothing onto world markets from the 1950s and 1960s onwards (see chart below). Even with penal tariffs imposed by the Multifiber Arrangement (MFA), they succeeded in undercutting textiles made in traditional centers like Britain.

Textiles have historically been central to the whole process of industrial development. Partly this is because making fabrics is labor-intensive, partly because as a basic necessity there is always a strong local market for clothing, and partly because the technology required is not too sophisticated. Famously, even in the early 19th century, India still possessed a huge textiles industry, in many respects far superior to that in Britain. The Raj, however, put an end to this industry and substituted imports from Britain.

The pattern of exports from the NICs from the mid-1960s to the mid-1990s shows how they moved on and others took over. First exports from Hong Kong, Korea, Taiwan and Singapore rose sharply as a proportion of their total trade. Then they began to decline as more sophisticated industries (electronics and computers especially) took over. In their place, textile exports from Thailand and Indonesia rose sharply – though the Southeast Asian crash of 1997 left a question mark as to whether they would really be able to follow the original NICs onto the 'next step on the ladder'.

This is the model for 'export-led growth' that the World Bank and International Monetary Fund claim to have been following around the world. What this model does not accommodate, however, is export growth led by primary commodities in the majority of the world's poorest countries – which hasn't prevented the model being promoted regardless. ∎

Textiles, clothing and footwear exports from Newly Industrializing Countries

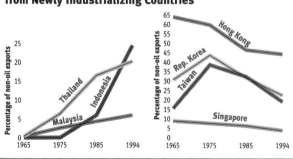

Trade and Development Report, 1996, UNCTAD.

103

Blue jeans

The brand I began with, way back in the mid-1960s, was Levi's. Levi Strauss & Co – the world's largest garment company – has a benevolent reputation. It withdrew production contracts from Burma and China because of human-rights violations. When it discovered child labor at one of its contractors in Bangladesh it did not throw the children onto the streets, but offered education instead. It made great play of retaining garment factories with recognized trade unions in the US. It devised and implemented what was once widely regarded as a model corporate code of business ethics.

Relative to union-busting, sex-toting 'labels' like Guess? Inc – which is more representative of the generality of labels – Levi's looks positively saintly, not to say smug. Perhaps it can afford to be, charging as it does a healthy premium for the 'cult' status of its jeans.

Levi's in China
Still, Levi's is a long way from perfect. It has shown little serious interest in organic cotton and alternative fibers. It will not allow independent monitoring of its code, which makes it worth very little. Then came massive job losses in the US – and a return to China.

Clarence Grebey of Levi Strauss, explained: 'It is a business decision based on our belief that we can now identify business partners in mainland China who will comply with our strict codes of conduct. If that's not the case, we will not do business there.'

Harry Wu, the US human-rights activist, responded: 'What's improved in China is the business climate. In fact, human-rights violations are getting worse. Forced labor is still used in the garment industry. There are no independent unions and anyone who tries to organize workers would end up in a re-education camp.'

On balance, I feel more inclined to take the word of Harry Wu than Clarence Grebey.

So, between the big companies that dominate the jeans market, the choice is entirely relative. Among the worst is Guess? Inc. Because US garment workers, and their union UNITE, have promoted a boycott of Guess products, no-one in their right mind would touch them. Among the best, even now, is Levi's. But globalized 'cheap' labor and industrial cotton are integral to all of them. Corporate codes of conduct have their limitations. Business is business.

So I turned to the ecological front – studiously ignored by the big companies – where, to begin with, things looked a little more encouraging. The Internet threw up several suppliers of organic-cotton jeans, but they were sold only in North America. Panda, the catalogue of World Wide Fund for Nature (WWF), Zurich, offered 'Bio-Damensjeans "Girls' Fit"'.

I had also heard rumors that the original jeans were made from hemp, a fiber more usually associated with rope and sacks. There is a dedicated band of devotees who claim that hemp doesn't need pesticides and has 25,000 different uses: the war on drugs (yes, hemp is the source of marijuana) might be a scam by vested cotton interests to scupper a dangerous rival. Then the Body Shop launched a new line in hemp cosmetics – immediately condemned and therefore promoted by the drugs warriors – which made it feel like safer territory for me.

Hemp jeans

On the Internet again I found hemp jeans from Romania priced at $60 – but, once more, available only in the US. In a catalogue there was a pair priced at $150 – too extravagant for me. I set an upper limit for myself of $100 – steep enough, but at least in the same bracket as 'designer' labels. Then, through Ethical Consumer magazine, I found the Hemp Union of Hull, and Dick Bye on the other end of the phone.

Yes, he said, Hemp Union sold blue jeans at $100.

Blue jeans

In fact, he sent me a pair in 'natural' color. They were lovely – softer and floppier than denim, like linen but tougher, warmer. There were very fetching, distinctive green leaves on the label, which said: 'If you try to smoke the garment you will get nothing but an awful headache. Save the Planet!'

What about the claim that Hemp Union products were 'manufactured without exploitation'? Well, said Dick Bye, the jeans were made for a company in Denmark by a manufacturer in – China. The PC pair was, he said, perfectly feasible, but would cost more than three times as much, 'and we don't feel that the current market would stand this'.

Who pays the price?

I thought about this for a minute. If poison- and sweat-free jeans cost $300, who pays for the $50 pair? Why, the human environment and those young women in sweatshops, of course. In effect, they provide a subsidy to consumers. Think about this a little more, and you realize that if producers were paid more, so that they themselves could afford to buy fairly traded products that in turn cost less, and you'd be moving in the right direction – and in almost precisely the opposite direction from current orthodoxy.

The fact is, however, that the perfectly PC pair of jeans does not exist. We don't have that limitless choice after all. It is not just the image, but the promise, of consumer capitalism that lies.

As 'consumers' we do indeed have power. We should use it as constructively as we can, opting for the relatively good rather than the absolutely bad products.

This means thinking differently, reclaiming the substance of 'identity' from the silly labels that litter the marketplace, deriving some sense of satisfaction – rather than inconvenience – from the process. Of course, in the rich world at least, 'consumer' movements have been active for some time. So far as jeans are concerned they have yet to make much difference, though perhaps we should not be surprised. After all, no-one ever changed anything of importance just by buying something else – but we can make a difference by not buying, and protesting, as consumer groups in the South have shown. Meanwhile, the people who make jeans are busy figuring out how best to put things right. Eventually they must succeed, if only because humanity will not tolerate such shameful treatment for ever.

So too, and thanks to a small but growing band of pioneers, organic cotton and alternative fibers are within reach of offering a viable alternative to industrial cotton. In the end they, too, must succeed, because the earth will not tolerate such mistreatment indefinitely, either.

If we wait until the globalizers have run out of runway, however, a wreck is all we'll find at the end of it. A political response, and political support for the alternatives, is now required. That means weaving the two strands of ecology and social justice together. All too often they run in parallel, preoccupied by their own priorities. Each tends to look on the other as an extra burden, a different history. But when they are woven together then each will be made stronger by the other, and change will at last be possible.

In the meantime, what we do have is a sense of direction. Truth to tell, it's a much more attractive, far less suicidal route than the one we've been traveling so far. It's been mapped out for us by people who refuse to accept that nothing can be done and no-one is listening. All we have to do now is prove that they are right.

6 Buying it: fair trade in the North

A journey through the world of chocolateers and chocoholics with a Ghanaian cocoa farmer.

Eventually, fair trade reaches its final destination – the consuming societies of the North. It is here that, on average, 90 per cent or more of its value stays. There's a limit to what fair trade can do about this. So great is the dominance of an ever-smaller number of ever-larger retail chains that fair trade can't hope to reach the majority of people in any other way than from their shelves. It isn't yet big enough to sustain its own processing industries – ripening bananas, roasting coffee, grinding cocoa – and so has to rely on finding the few independent companies that are willing to do this for it, which doesn't come cheap.

Short of fair trade getting very much bigger it's not easy to see a way out of this. One of the great assets of Alternative Trading Organizations (ATOs) is that they do indeed create different retail systems – charity shops or 'direct selling' networks like Traidcraft in Britain or Equal Exchange in the US. If farmers' markets and neighborhood retailing initiatives can keep a foot in the door, then they – like the co-operative wholesale societies – do provide a sizable addition. But for the time being, if fair trade is to be a reliable option for a significant number of producers, there is no alternative but to fight for its space on supermarket shelves, where volume is the better part of value. Generating that volume, in turn, means resorting to marketing campaigns and 'brand awareness'. Before you know it – and if you're not very careful indeed – fair trade takes on an uncomfortably close resemblance to any other trade.

Well, fair-traders are used to getting their hands dirty and still keeping clean. In some ways their 'entryism' is more subversive than staying forever on the outside looking in. The risks involved are enormous, and doubtless there will be casualties that simply sink back into the mainstream. But there is one thing that makes this less likely, and that is the direct, personal links fair-traders have with producers. Try following the fair-trade path with them, rather than with their products, and the difference is clear from the start – as Richard Swift discovered when he came to Britain with a cocoa farmer from Ghana.

'What is a cocoa farmer who has never been out of his country before doing coming to the United Kingdom?' On the surface of it, a reasonable enough question. It was the imperious manner of the immigration officer that gave it its intimidating weight. Koto Asamoah Serebour stood looking very small and uncertain in his only good suit. A cocoa farmer, he had showed me what cocoa means to many Ghanaians. Now it was time to return the hospitality and show him the chocolate-consuming business in Britain. It was six in the morning at London's Gatwick Airport. No-one was in a good mood.

The first barrier

I went back to see if I could help. The immigration officer was incredulous. I had naively assumed that once we had won the battle with the British High Commission in Accra it would be plain sailing. But Asamoah had at first been refused his visa and those clever devils at the High Commission had stamped the refusal right in his passport. At six in the morning at Gatwick Airport that was like a red flag to a bull.

Pretty tame stuff, compared to what many people have to put up with crossing borders, but the Athenian disdain of the voice of authority was still irksome. It was not just a question of Asamoah's skin color but also of his style. He lacked the self-assurance of the globalized robots who run the world economy and pass through immigration like a subway turnstile.

Fair trade in the North

Authority smells a lack of confidence like a Rottweiler smells fear.

Eventually the fact that Asamoah already had his visa got us through. But it was plain that this was an unusual and unwelcome state of affairs. It was okay for Asamoah's cocoa beans to travel to Britain, but he was expected to stay at home. It is one of the central ironies of the global economy – freedom for commodities and capital but not for people.

The idea was that we would try and get a look at various aspects of chocolate production and consumption. We had been warned that this would not be that easy, as big chocolate manufacturers are notoriously secretive about letting people tour their facilities. Our first refusal came from the good folks at Mars, who didn't want Asamoah to see how they made Mars Bars in Slough. Similarly, Cadbury's expressed skepticism when we approached them – even their trade union was reluctant to let us meet members to compare working lives in factories with those in the field. Undaunted, we pressed on.

Fair-traders

We went to London to meet the people at Twin Trading, the organization that supports small-scale farmers' access to markets. Here we got a good overview of what is being done by way of fair trade, as well as information about the cocoa trade and the politics and economics of Big Chocolate. The 'chocolate man' at Twin Trading was Simon Wright, who had become disillusioned working in the mainstream chocolate industry, where he was employed trying to reduce the already small amount of cocoa solids in the commercial British product.

Simon traced for Asamoah the route that cocoa takes to get to market. All of it passes through the Dutch port of Rotterdam and then is processed by Dutch Cocoa into either cocoa liquor, butter or powder. It then becomes the key ingredient for chocolate manufactured in several locations in continental Europe. The fair-trade chocolate is made in either Switzerland or Germany with the cocoa butter being used as a base for cosmetics.

Probably not very much of Ghana's cocoa ever made it into the huge British chocolate market. The best cocoa fetches a premium price that only high-grade chocolate manufacturers are willing to pay. Most British factories are not even set up to make high-grade chocolate. The opinion at Twin was that not much in the way of high-quality chocolate gets produced anywhere in the English-speaking world. Big Chocolate, which dominates the English (Cadburys, Mars and Nestlé) and the US (Hershey, Kraft, Mars and Nestlé again) markets, is more interested in a low-cost product than in high-quality chocolate with lots of cocoa solids. The average content of the leading market products is in the 20-per-cent range, whereas good European chocolate comes in closer to 40 or 50 per cent.

A rough, back-of-the-envelope calculation, based on a cocoa price of about $1,750 a ton, revealed that on a market-leading chocolate bar that sells at about $1.80 in the shops, a cocoa producer could expect to see about three cents.

Good chocolate

'Historically, the English have not wanted their chocolate to taste much like chocolate,' said Simon. 'Indeed, they haven't gone for any strong flavors at all. When you bite into most English commercial chocolate, the first sensation is a sweetish toffee kind of taste.'

But the interest in quality and safe food that is sweeping the Anglo-Saxon world may mean a brighter future for good chocolate. For fair trade the best option may lie in producing high-quality chocolate that uses lots of cocoa (with no chemical inputs) and returns a decent price to the farmer. This would allow the product to be marketed with an appeal to quality and health as well as fairness.

Twin's big success story had been Cafédirect, their widely distributed ground coffee. The launch of Divine in 1998 added a strong, popular-tasting brand to the main fair-traded chocolate brands marketed on the continent, where fair-trade cocoa volumes are rising.

By and large, fair-traded chocolate has been slower to get off the ground than coffee. It proved hard to break the stranglehold of Big Chocolate, who are able to keep the price low and saturate the media with brand-identification advertising. If you want to do it differently everything costs more – more for raw materials, smaller more expensive batch runs in smaller factories. However, the chocolate market is so large and lucrative that even a very small market niche could mean a lot of money and a lot of cocoa. The arrival of Divine and, in 2000, of Dubble (for children) took fair trade to the corner shop, the gas station and the cinema for the first time, backed by an educational link to Comic Relief and teachers.

Speculative purchase

Our next stop after Twin was the trading floor of the London Futures Market (LIIF). Here Asamoah was very surprised that in the place devoted to buying and selling cocoa there was not a bean in sight. The level of abstraction involved with futures trading was hard for either of us to grasp. The scene was like something out of the film Wall Street. But the screaming and wild gesticulating of the traders in the pit seemed to Asamoah to be little more than 'a group of madmen' whose purpose was mysterious and obscure.

Our guides were at great pains to explain to us the underlying rationality of the trading system, despite its complexity. They pointed out that, unlike the New York futures market where there is much more pure speculation, 70 to 80 per cent of the buying and selling in London is based on 'physicals'. By this we took them to mean that contracts for the delivery of cocoa are mostly done by people in the industry (shippers, big trading houses, processors or manufacturers) with only 20 to 30 per cent done by those who have absolutely nothing to do with cocoa – the pure speculators. The big chocolate companies are mostly represented by stand-in buyers so that their ultimate 'demand' intentions remain disguised. The purpose of the market for those in the industry is to 'lock in' prices as a hedge against unexpected increases. This is understandable enough in a volatile market, where prices have been known to be as high as $4,800 a ton, and as low as $800.

Yo-yo prices

So far, so good. But only two to three per cent of these futures contracts at the exchange ever end up in the physical delivery of cocoa. Indeed, seven or eight times (even higher in New York) more cocoa is bought and sold on the exchange than exists or ever will exist in the world. Contracts are being bought and sold nearly two years in advance. This sounded to me like speculation, no matter who was doing it.

Most actual deals for the physical delivery of beans are done by fax or over the telephone between the different players in the industry, by-passing the exchange entirely. Yet the exchange remains crucial in setting the price. A lot of people do very well indeed out of the futures market. One must be forgiven for the fleeting idea that this speculation is being done on the backs of hard-pressed producers who actually grow the beans, without whom this whole edifice would crumble. If there is this much money to be made in cocoa, why should it be so hard for Asamoah to get enough from his crop to pay the school fees for his youngest son in Kumasi? Of course more sane

The cocoa chain

A chocolate bar may look like a fairly simple thing to you. But, even after the bean has been grown, dried and dispatched from producers' countries like Ghana, it still has an extremely complex process to go through before it becomes a bar of chocolate – and then it has to be wrapped and distributed to retail outlets like supermarkets. These are the links between cocoa and chocolate, including the main corporations involved at the beginning – and the end of the chain. ∎

The links that bind cocoa to chocolate

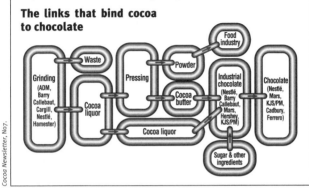

Cocoa Newsletter, No7.

ways of balancing supply and demand are not popular in this market-mad era with its demands to 'liberalize' everything.

Craig Sams' Whole Earth Foods produced Green and Black's organic chocolate. Fair-trade Maya Gold was made with cocoa from a co-operative in Belize. Sams had a broad vision of the political economy of food and a special interest in cocoa and chocolate. He saw the richness, flavor and individuality of good chocolate as tied to the unique care small farmers give to the variety of their trees and beans. He was certain this would never be replicated in the uniformity of plantation agriculture: 'Nothing in the world has such a complexity of flavors. There are over 400 distinct smells that come from the cocoa bean – the rose has only 14 and the onion just 6 or 7.'

Sams found it distressing that cocoa was the world's

most heavily sprayed food crop.

But he believed that the small farmer was ultimately the most efficient producer of beans. 'Plantations can only compete if they are run under conditions of slave labor, with extremely low wages – and people will only put up with that for so long.' The dramatic drop in the share of cocoa production from Brazilian and Malaysian plantations supported Sams' argument. An epidemic of Witches Broom disease on Brazilian plantations had shown the way genetic uniformity undermines agro-chemical crops.

Small means efficient

But if small is an advantage in cocoa production, it is not so in chocolate retailing. Sams had a hard time breaking into the huge British chocolate market. A combination of saturation advertising, clout with buyers and cheap production made Big Chocolate a fierce competitor. Nonetheless, Green and Black's sales had been growing by 20 to 30 per cent a year.

Asamoah was quick to see the sales opportunity and asked if Sams had any place for his own beans from the Kuapa co-operative in Ghana. Sams was sympathetic, but would require them to be certified organic. Asamoah pondered the possibility. Later, as we toured some organic shops in London's West End, he became increasingly intrigued by the idea of Kuapa 'going organic'. He, like so many other Ghanaian farmers, had already cut down on chemical pesticides because of the expense. It might be difficult to convince other Kuapa members to cut out the cheaper, less toxic fungicides used against the devastating Black Pod disease. But Asamoah was beginning to think this could be the wave of the future: 'I think that everything that we sell should be organic. Otherwise we will be left behind and not able to sell our cocoa.'

Sad, therefore, to have to report that in May 2005 Green and Black's shocked its customers by selling out to Big Chocolate: Cadbury Schweppes swallowed it whole in a deal reportedly worth $30 million.

Asamoah and I ended our tour in the Big Chocolate game. Most chocolate companies – most food companies, for that matter – do not like groups of nosy customers wandering around their factories. So they have set up theme parks outside. The parks combine elements of the production process with a magical world where fantasy and history intersect in one glorious burst of self-promotion. We entered 'Cadbury World'.

The overwhelming impression was of sheer scale: one 12-hour shift packs 345,000 bars; 800 bars a minute; 12,000 tons a week. Despite chocolate's reputation as a luxurious food, for Big Chocolate it is, first and foremost, an industrial product. Although many of the operations in Cadbury World were still done by hand, in the real plant everything is automated. The idea is to give the customer the sense that Big Chocolate still regards chocolate-making as a craft, carried out under the 'watchful eyes of our most experienced chocolateers', who never tire of the stuff: 'They are chocoholics. Chocolate is a way of life.'

Asamoah felt he'd rather work under his trees than on the line for Cadbury. He introduced himself to one younger worker and asked about the use of Ghanaian cocoa. The worker said that he thought most of the cocoa came from Malaysia.

Cadbury World takes the customer through a sanitized history of cocoa – no slaves here – to a 'craft-like' sample of chocolate-making, then a revealing survey of advertising around the world and over the decades. It all ends with a Disneyesque fantasy ride in little cars through a place called Beanville, where one meets such characters as the Bean Team and Mister Chunky Choc. The iconography is perfect – industry prying loose Third World raw materials, slapping them on the assembly line and then convincing the gullible that their purchase is a magic route to a fantasy happiness. In Spain the ads are set to flamenco guitar; in the US it is cutesy mini-egg bunnies.

For Asamoah, amazement was clearly the main reaction. It was a long way down the cocoa chain from his eight acres in Ghana. The concerns of Big

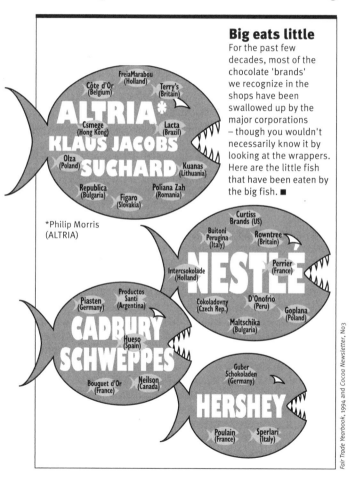

Big eats little

For the past few decades, most of the chocolate 'brands' we recognize in the shops have been swallowed up by the major corporations – though you wouldn't necessarily know it by looking at the wrappers. Here are the little fish that have been eaten by the big fish. ∎

FreiaMarabou (Holland)
Côte d'Or (Belgium)
Terry's (Britain)
ALTRIA*
Csmege (Hong Kong)
Lacta (Brazil)
KLAUS JACOBS
Olza (Poland)
SUCHARD
Kuanas (Lithuania)
Republica (Bulgaria)
Figaro (Slovakia)
Poliana Zah (Romania)

*Philip Morris (ALTRIA)

Curtiss Brands (US)
Buitoni Perugina (Italy)
Rowntree (Britain)
Intercsokolade (Holland)
NESTLÉ
Perrier (France)
Cokoladovny (Czech Rep.)
D'Onofrio (Peru)
Maltschika (Bulgaria)
Goplana (Poland)

Productos Santi (Argentina)
Piasten (Germany)
CADBURY SCHWEPPES
Hueso (Spain)
Bouquet d'Or (France)
Neilson (Canada)

Guber Schokoladen (Germany)
HERSHEY
Poulain (France)
Sperlari (Italy)

Fair Trade Yearbook, 1994 and Cocoa Newsletter, No3

Fair trade in the North

Chocolate to cut costs while increasing market share were a universe away from the struggle of West African farmers for a minimal well-being based on a decent price for their beans.

But there are markets and markets. In the vast Kumasi market in Ghana, where Asamoah's daughter Gloria sells her tomatoes and onions, you can buy almost anything, but no chocolate or even cocoa beans. These markets are quite different from the long-distance export markets that trade cocoa before the pods even sprout from the trees. A drought may shift prices dramatically, but ultimately it is the projections of demand and supply by Big Chocolate,

Unequal exchange

A recurrent theme in the 'commercialization' of all Southern commodities in the North is the way it is controlled by a very small number of very large transnational corporations. Add to this the growing power of the big retail chains – like Wal-Mart – and you begin to understand the near-monopoly or 'oligopoly' with which corporations ensure that the system operates in their interests. So long as they control one end of the trade – increasingly the 'consumer' end – then they can be pretty sure of deciding what goes on at the other, 'producer', end as well. The notion that world trade promotes ruthless competition is pure fiction. Corporations share more common interests than they have bones of contention.

So we can find very similar patterns of control across a range of commodities, from coffee to chocolate and bananas. A relatively new pattern is, however, also beginning to emerge. The risks associated with actual production are large, and the rewards are not very great. In this way the big corporations have been shifting their control away from production, which they are increasingly content to leave to small or 'independent' producers. In the end, these producers will, nonetheless, have to sell to the corporations anyway, and it is here, in the commercialization

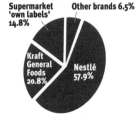

Concentration of control

Coffee (market share, Britain)

Supermarket 'own labels' 14.8%

Other brands 6.5%

Kraft General Foods 20.8%

Nestlé 57.9%

using all the paraphernalia of modern research technology and commercial calculations, that decide price. It's a contest of unequals, with the end buyer and seller barely even aware of each other's existence. The difference in life-experience between a dealer on the New York Commodity Exchange with a six-figure salary, and someone who owns a small cocoa farm in West Africa, is too vast to contemplate. Yet gaining competitive position for one may put the very survival of the other into question.

African markets are not like this. Here people look each other in the eye, discuss the quality of the goods, what is fair and what each party can afford. If

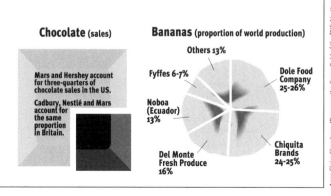

and 'branding' of products, that they now concentrate their efforts.

The pattern varies slightly from one product to the next. Bananas arrive in refrigerated 'reefer' ships and, short of being ripened for sale, require very little attention; they receive their corporate 'brand' directly on the skin. Coffee requires a little more processing through roasting and blending (and freeze-drying for 'instant' coffee), so the brand goes onto the jar, and this is where corporate power kicks in. Chocolate is more complex, requiring other ingredients (sugar, milk, fats) and frequently is further manufactured into heavily promoted bars, biscuits and candies. At one crucial stage or another, however, big corporations intervene in every product before it eventually reaches the final consumer. ■

Chocolate (sales)

Mars and Hershey account for three-quarters of chocolate sales in the US.

Cadbury, Nestlé and Mars account for the same proportion in Britain.

Bananas (proportion of world production)

Others 13%

Fyffes 6-7%

Dole Food Company 25-26%

Noboa (Ecuador) 13%

Chiquita Brands 24-25%

Del Monte Fresh Produce 16%

Anne Claire Chambron, 'Bananas: the Green Gold of the TNCs' in *Hungry for Power*, UK Food Group, London, March 1999.

the product doesn't meet expectations the buyer can return to complain directly. If the seller thinks the price offered is just too low there are usually other customers willing to pay a reasonable price. Prices more or less fit the needs of human survival. There is honesty and equality here. So when next you hear the 'free market' being lionized, make sure to inquire which market the speaker has in mind.

Boosting fair trade

Serious efforts are being made to introduce fairness into international trade. These are closely tied to the production of high-quality chocolate. Farmers' co-ops like Kuapa, fair-traders like Twin Trading and fair-trade producers like Divine and a number of others – mostly in continental Europe – are leading the way. In Canada and the US you can get Masaco chocolate from Bolivian cocoa; in Australia it's Force 10 from Samoan cocoa, and Trade Aid chocolate in Aotearoa/New Zealand. But a better price for cocoa remains far down the priority list of Big Chocolate, where trends are the same as those throughout the global corporate economy: merger mania, restructuring to reduce costs, and the battle for market share, mostly through heavily advertised, low-cocoa-content chocolate bars and candies.

Building an alternative unites the battle for fairness with that for a quality – often more healthy and organic – product. One way of giving a leg-up to fair-trade goods would be by reducing the sales tax on them. In an era that glorifies the unfettered market this is bound to be greeted with screams of 'unfair subsidy'. Yet, for example, agricultural subsidies in Europe are estimated to add nearly $36 to the average family food bill every week. And, in the era of supposed free trade, Ghana's excellent chocolate would meet a 34-per-cent tariff if it ever reached a European port.

Things may not be all bleak for small producers. There is an emerging consensus that the small farm is the best way to produce cocoa as well as to preserve biodiversity. But all is not rosy for them either. The shifting pattern of production in Ghana has moved from east to west as soil fertility declines and trees age. Even small farmers face problems unless the best of grassroots science – integrated pest management, new ideas in inter-cropping, soil science – is made available to them. Who will be there to do this if structural-adjustment policies cut agricultural-outreach services to the bone, as they have done in Ghana?

If small farmers are to be the wave of the future they must do better out of a chocolate bar. Big Chocolate won't jump on its own – pressure is needed. On the political side, some of this is beginning to come from the 'Cocoa Platforms': alliances of unions, producers, fair-traders, environmentalists and other activists in the industry in Europe, Brazil and Ghana.

Economic pressure must also come from those who produce a higher-quality, cocoa-intensive product. If dissatisfaction grows with the cocoa-poor, sugar-heavy candy that Big Chocolate passes off on a public unaware of the alternatives, the market niche for better-quality chocolate will expand.

Meanwhile – particularly for children, who do not like 'dark' chocolate at all – the arrival of boisterous fair-trade alternatives in mass markets ensures they aren't confined entirely to a 'niche'. Even a small drop in market share is something big companies cannot afford to ignore.

So, as the political hucksters are fond of saying, this is a 'win-win scenario': good for farmers, good for consumers, good for the ecosystem. Don't feel guilty – buy fair trade and have another bite.

7 Fair Trade's future: an infant among giants

Though fair trade may be an infant among giants, the future lies with the infant, not the giant.

THE HUMBUG OF foul trade is obvious, but powerful interests keep it in place, a bedraggled ideological shield for corporate globalization.

Meanwhile, the fair trade movement has grown a good deal faster than some of us anticipated, and for at least two good reasons. The first is the global justice movement, which has given the trading system a critical presence in the public mind that was once hard to envisage. The second is the improved range, quality and availability of fair trade products, which offer a very scarce commodity indeed: something practical that almost anyone can do to counteract injustice.

Together they have created a small but growing space 'in and against the market', where unorthodox experiments can prosper despite an increasingly fundamentalist mainstream. Each has, by accident or design, helped to enlarge the possibilities of the other and enhance the fair trade movement.

Separately, however, they pull in opposite directions, the one towards a niche in a market that the other aims to transform. On their own – one might say 'in or against the market' – they are far weaker. And there are now some worrying signs that they may be pulling apart. Approaching adolescence, the fair trade infant is having to face some awkward dilemmas.

'We aspire to grow and therefore we want more funds,' said Penny Newman, Managing Director of Britain's biggest fair trade coffee company, CaféDirect, announcing its floatation on financial markets in 2004. 'We are a commercial venture, not a charity,' added Sylvie Barr, CaféDirect's Head of Strategic Development, as if to reassure potential investors, who

The growth of fair trade

Though still a minute fraction of total world trade, fair trade has been growing fast – and accelerating.

• In Britain, sales of goods carrying the Fairtrade Foundation label increased in value from $31 million in 1998 to $174 million in 2003.

• In Switzerland, 50% of bananas consumed now carry the 'Fairtrade' label.

• Worldwide, sales of 'Fairtrade' labelled goods increased from 26,920 metric tons in 1997 to 83,480 metric tons in 2003 – with an increase of 42.3% between 2002 and 2003 alone.

• After its launch at the World Social Forum in January 2004, the Fair Trade Organization Mark was adopted by more than 140 producer groups worldwide. ■

Sources: www.fairtrade.net, www.ifat.org

were being offered control of the company.[1]

Then came an announcement from the Fairtrade Foundation, which authenticates Britain's 'Fairtrade' label. It was being awarded to Tesco, Britain's biggest retailer, for a new line of flowers from Kenya. 'Tesco is renowned for understanding its customers,' claimed Ian Bretman, Commercial Director of the Fairtrade Foundation, in a Tesco press release. 'This is good news for producers, who will benefit from the additional sales, and good news for consumers, who will see a much greater choice of quality Fairtrade products in stores.'[2]

Good news all round, then. Well, maybe. Floating on financial markets is, after all, a tricky business at the best of times and certainly not renowned for its fairness. Tesco, on the other hand, is renowned for a good deal more than 'understanding its customers' – screwing down producers and running everyone else out of town, for instance.

So has the mainstream miraculously changed course – diverted, perhaps, by the fair trade movement? A degree of hubris is required to believe this and the hard evidence suggests otherwise. In 2003 some supermarkets in Britain were accused of overcharging for fair trade products. They were, it was claimed, retaining much of the premium on the price for themselves. Tesco was among the stores reportedly marking up fair trade bananas by as much as one US dollar per kilogram – more than double the premium going to producers. Whether or not the allegations were true, these supermarkets were evidently in a position to place the 'Fairtrade' label in jeopardy of losing much of its hard-earned credibility.[3]

Such developments in Britain were, as ever, fore-shadowed in the US. In 2000 TransFair USA provided certification for the Starbucks chain of coffee shops, saying: 'With every cup of Starbucks Fair Trade coffee, consumers are supporting and empowering farmers and their families.'[4] What, then, would they be doing with the very much larger proportion of conventional cups of coffee most of them would go on buying from this icon of corporate globalization?

Transfair USA was duly followed by Oxfam UK, which received from Starbucks a donation of $188,000 towards a rural development program in Ethiopia, in exchange for some sort of 'collaboration' on the crisis in the world coffee trade.[5]

Meanwhile, at an international level the Fairtrade Labelling Organization (FLO), based in Germany, is floating the possibility of the 'Big Banana' companies using the Fairtrade label. FLO has teamed up with Dole to certify some of its banana sales in Europe. Chiquita now asserts that nearly half its bananas meet the requirements of Social Accountability International, which claims to certify 'humane' working conditions worldwide.[6]

Slippery slope
This is a very slippery slope indeed. The fair trade claim to fairness is, after all, only relative – it is fairer than the mainstream, not completely fair in every respect. If the claim is eroded, the fair trade movement

could very easily find itself promoting a larger and larger volume of increasingly foul trade, until the last trace of any real difference vanished altogether.

These and related issues have now become the focus of vigorous debate within the International Federation of Alternative Trade (IFAT), the main umbrella group for fair trade producers, importers and retailers. If the labellers pursue their current course, and lose any clear connection with what makes fair trade different, then the distinctiveness of producers may become the defining element of fair trade. The infant heir to the future is then more likely to be Southern producers than Northern consumers.

After all, give a 'Fairtrade' label to Tesco, Starbucks or Dole and there's no reason to deny it to the likes of, say, Nestlé. This Swiss-based transnational corporation is – among other things, including the persistent promotion of baby milk to mothers who don't need it and have no means of using it safely – the world's largest coffee manufacturing business. So surely, using the same logic, something like a 'Fairtrade' Nestlé coffee brand would be even better news all round.

Foul trade

You have to know a little about how foul trade works in order to figure out why not. The price of commodities like coffee that corporations buy from producers in the South has been in long-term decline. The reasons for this relate more closely than is generally recognized to the debt mechanism, which forces bankrupt Southern countries to export whatever basic commodities they can, all at once. The result is a glut on world markets which causes prices to fall.

However, the retail prices paid by consumers in the North have not fallen in parallel – a theoretical impossibility in a 'free' market and a sure sign of monopolistic forces at work. That leaves an unanswered question. Where can the difference have gone, other than into the ample coffers of the likes of Nestlé? The amounts of money routinely stolen in this way, from producers and consumers alike, are so huge as to dwarf the relatively meagre recompense offered by fair trade.

Nestlé has evidently felt under some sort of obligation to account for this. In Britain rumours circulated in 2004 that the giant was about to give birth to its very own infant, a rogue 'fair trade' coffee brand that would circumvent the usual authenticating process and confuse the issue as much as possible.[7]

Nestlé's public posture towards fair trade has, indeed, always been hostile. The basic problem, it insists, is 'too many beans'. By defying market forces, paying a higher price to producers and thereby encouraging more coffee beans to be produced, fair trade actually makes matters worse. The answer? Coffee farmers must 'diversify' – do something, anything, completely different.[8]

Other options

What, exactly, might that be? If other options were readily available, does Nestlé imagine that coffee farmers would not have jumped at them already? Desperate farmers are just as likely to respond to falling prices by trying to produce more, in an attempt to maintain their subsistence-level incomes.

That is precisely what official, 'structural adjustment' or 'poverty reduction' programmes have enforced via the debt mechanism. Is Nestlé really unaware of this?

The corporation offers only one choice. The world price of coffee must fall further, until... well, one can only presume, until coffee farmers starve to death and are finally rendered incapable of producing any more beans. Why would Nestlé want the trade to operate otherwise, since the corporation plays such a prominent part in making it as it is?

In any event, the Tescos, Starbucks and Nestlés of this world are by their nature more interested in profits from the premium on the retail price than in the principles of fair trade. The premium is not, however, one of the principles. These are about changing the relationship between producers and consumers.

If big business really were interested in change it would stop stealing from producers, restore to them some of the retail price differential it currently pockets – and charge consumers no premium for fair trade at all.

That would, at a stroke, open up fair trade to those who are deterred by the premium, hugely increasing its 'market share' as a result. But it would also remove the price advantage of exploitative trade and transform the entire system, with profound implications for corporate profitability – which is, of course, why no such thing is ever proposed.

For their part, customers in the North may readily assume – as with charity – that the fair trade premium goes straight to producers in the 'Third World'. A simple appeal, but not always or even entirely true. For example, in the rare and usually brief event of the coffee price rising sharply – say, a frost cuts production in Brazil – 'Fairtrade' contracts might pay less to producers than the market price, in exchange for a guarantee always to buy above the 'cost of production'. This cost is set by local subsistence levels and has nothing remotely to do with prosperity for producers.

Relatively arcane considerations, perhaps. But the fact that fairness is relative and complex militates against the simple 'unique selling point' required by a label, and leaves the 'brand image' of fair trade inherently vulnerable to discredit. Questions of trust and intent are involved here. And if people can trust the intent of Tesco, Starbucks, Dole, Nestlé and financial markets, why bother with fair trade?

Fair Trade's future

Not just winning trust

Besides, fair trade is not just about winning the trust of consumers. Producers too have to be convinced of its value, in circumstances where the very survival of entire communities may be at stake. Among other things, that means demonstrating the real difference between fair and foul trade, establishing long-term, reliable relationships and showing how, through all the machinations of the market, there really is an alternative that works – not just a marginal difference from a system that remains in most other respects exactly the same.

Economic orthodoxy makes great play of its ability to divide the world very neatly in two; credit and debit, asset and liability, profit and loss, supply and demand, producer and consumer. It asserts that the two tend towards some kind of balance or 'equilibrium', though this it cannot actually prove from the historical record. In practice, consumer capitalism invariably heads for the nearest crisis, veering wildly towards slump or boom, depression or elation – characteristics that in people would be symptomatic of a manic form of madness.

Caught in the untidy ambiguities of daily life, however, real people are neither consumers nor producers, never entirely one thing or the other, always both at the same time. Without producers there would, after all, be nothing to consume – and no-one to consume it. If the customer were always right and the consumer sovereign, over whom, precisely, would they exercise their sovereignty?

In its essence, fair trade is not a brand with passive consumers but a movement with active supporters – a relationship of trust and solidarity between people. These people show what is possible and make an informed statement about the mainstream. They defy the imperative to buy cheap and ignore the consequences. They offer a trace of respect to just a few of the many millions of producers whom foul trade routinely humiliates.

Like people, fair trade relies on complex networks. So it depends on wider movements – like the continuing campaign to dismantle the odious debt mechanism that has such a direct impact on the way trade works. There are close links between trade and the environment as well. The industrial food trade, for example, hasn't just poisoned, displaced or impoverished many millions of producers in hungry countries; it has adulterated the food chain and created a series of environmental disasters into the bargain. There is every reason why 'fair' must eventually also mean 'green' – food, clothing, computers, energy, anything you care to name.

Labor movement

Another link is to the labor movement. Central to the whole process of unfair trade has been its ability to move capital around the world in search of cheap labor. This has prompted a reaction from some trade unions and populist politicians in the North. They have looked to their national governments to provide protection from the loss of employment and the assault on working conditions that 'runaway' jobs in the South seem to represent. Support for this position has also come from some corporations, seeking to protect their investments in the North and justify very profitable government subsidies, particularly in agriculture.

Understandable though it may seem, this reaction is misguided. The most urgent priority is surely to strengthen the labor movement worldwide, and in particular to enforce the basic standards of employment agreed by the International Labor Organization (ILO). Perhaps there is some confusion here. What this means in practice is often as basic as the right of labor to organize at all. There were powerful objec-

The net works

Michael Barratt Brown, whose work has been instrumental in the development of fair trade, sketches a few outlines of what the future might look like.

At the lowest level of the housing estate or village, groups would form elected community councils. These would then have responsibility for certain services – cleaning, gardening, plumbing and minor building repairs – for which they could make a charge, and also for renting out premises for workshops and retail outlets, shops and restaurants, from which they would receive an income to use as they saw fit, to improve the environment, for recreation grounds, parks, crèches, etc. Through horizontal linkages they would network with similar estates and blocks of flats in wards and districts, including the surrounding countryside, both to provide appropriate services in housing, health, education, garbage collection, footpaths, swimming pools, parks and playing fields, and so draw upon those enterprises producing for local needs – fruit and vegetables, bakeries, housing materials, etc. Contracts and prices would then be the subject of negotiation on quality and service between representatives of the workers, the groups of households and the elected local authority at district level. The authorities would also need to obtain supplies from outside the district. This could be done by building links with enterprises whose products suited their needs. By adding here the element of networking, these links could be strengthened into continuing relationships allowing for forward planning beyond a single purchase or contract. This happens now, where public purchasing officers have found suppliers that they can rely on to understand their special needs. District authorities could also help to finance specialized networks, such as ethnic minorities, who want to develop provision for their own particular needs and tastes. These could include many of the organizations that are now involved in alternative trade.

In this model the communities and districts form the real building blocks of decentralized power, with their own elected councils and much-extended responsibilities. For it is at this level that people can meet each other and get to know each other's interests, share common facilities and feel a common responsibility for the care and protection of the neighborhood.

District and community councils can do much to strengthen social provision for all. But in the provision of personal and household needs we shall also have to bring a higher level of power to bear, where large numbers can be deployed to make up for individual financial weakness. Cities and counties comprise populations of several million and it is to them that we must look for the necessary power to influence household provision so that the needs of the poorer households are catered for.

At the level of the city and the county we are not only dealing with a much larger population and with health, education, police, fire brigades and public transport appropriate to the scale, but there will be productive enterprises, factories, mines and quarries, refineries and the like which have a national as well as an international market. It would be reasonable to imagine loosely, vertically integrated competing networks being based on cities and counties. In this case the power of a city or county authority would be enough to ensure that suppliers inside the network catered equally for the full range of income groups. Regional differences in income and tastes could then be allowed for. If cities and counties build up their own networks of suppliers, there is no reason why they should not link with neighboring cities and counties to widen their network.

When we reach the level of the nation-state, the question arises of the relationship between, on the one hand, the networks and the enterprises to which they are linked, and on the other, the arrangements to be made for allocating resources. Setting the parameters should surely be the limit of central responsibility, whether this is exercised by a state or federal body. For clearing the payments of international trade we have to envisage a much wider international structure than a federation.

Within these general parameters of resource allocation, networks should be free to make their own linkages and compete for business. The networks could not be said to be effective, competing traders if they could not set their own prices and make their own investments. If there were a great plurality of these networks for households to belong to, and if they were self-financing, not only enjoying the income of grants and subscriptions but also of their networking activities, they would have as much power as the giant companies today – but they would be subject to the democratic control of their members.

There remains the question of the relationship of the producing enterprises and the networks to the universal international system of resource allocation. Some of the enterprises may be quite large, supplying several, or even many, networks. They will want to have direct relations with the allocating center. Even if this is not a nation-state it will need to have the capacity to set norms for the operation of enterprises and to see that they are observed.

The great remaining problem is the necessity of imagining an international regulator and allocator of resources that does not replicate the bureaucracies of nation-states and of existing federations of states. Given the plurality of networks which is envisaged here, effective international representation of these networks, or of groups of networks, would have to be provided for. The setting of parameters for the operation of both networks and enterprises seems likely to imply something more continuous than occasional rounds of negotiation. One solution to this problem would be a world economic parliament, based on networks, a second Chamber of Peoples to complement the UN General Assembly, which is based on geographical nation-state constituencies. ∎

From Michael Barratt Brown, *Fair Trade*, Zed Books, London, 1993

tions to the entry of China into the WTO because of the absence of free trade unions in the Communist legacy. The repression of free trade unions in places like Guatemala, on the other hand, is routinely over-looked. There is a special kind of idiocy in the sugges-tion that free trade has a liberating effect in China, but is of no political consequence at all in Guatemala. A wider, global perspective has been slow to grow in the labor movement in the North, but it has always been there and is an obvious source of support for both the global justice and the fair trade movements.

For its part, the fair trade movement has yet to resolve its attitude to the labor movement. In theory, the right of labor to organize is one of the principles of fair trade. In practice, since many of its producers work in small co-operatives and relatively few for large conventional employers, the issue rarely arises. So there is little experience of the fair trade and labor movements collaborating to resolve some difficult issues. For example, if fair trade producers receive a guaranteed price above the cost of production, how does that translate into wage levels for employees? This, and issues like it, will not remain tangential for as long as fair trade grows.

Campus campaign

Meanwhile, a largely unreported student movement against sweatshop labor has been growing for some time on university campuses in the US and elsewhere. It has passed from one generation of students to the next, questioning the attitude of academic institutions towards increasingly pervasive corporate sponsorship. Nowhere is this more pronounced than in sports, where the globalization of the equipment industry and of corporate brands is almost complete. College sports are the seedbed of the whole process in the US. Yet in May 2000 Nike, stung by persistent campus criticism of its employment practices, started to withdraw its sponsorship from some college sports teams.

The anti-sweatshop movement in the US grew because it established a relationship with people and issues that are hard to ignore. In turn, it generated an interest in the wider world – such as what the WTO was up to in Seattle in November 1999. Here, for the first time on the streets of an American city, a generation of young Americans took issue with corporate America and the rigged rules of international trade.

Trade justice

A similar process had already been underway for some time in the South. The superficial signs of it are now visible, North and South, whenever corporate globalization puts on a public political face, at gatherings of the IMF, World Bank or WTO and at G8 summits. Despite the media focus on violent incidents, the extent of this resistance, particularly in the South and at huge events like the World Social Forum, goes almost entirely unreported by the Northern media. Nonetheless, as it knows to its cost, the corporate project now has to advance over contested ground almost everywhere. The gradual emergence of a global Trade Justice movement is, in this respect, the most hopeful possible sign for the long-term future of fair trade.

Meanwhile, a persistent search for imaginative alternatives and different ways of doing things remains as critical to the future of the fair trade movement as it has been to the core of its history so far. Not for nothing has its closest commercial ally in Britain been the Co-op. This huge co-operative, whose members are its customers, established the very first national retail chain in the country and has had deep roots in local communities since the 19th century. For all its subsequent failings, the Co-op is still answerable to its members, not to financial markets. Indeed, if the principles of fair trade encourage producers to work in co-operatives, why should not the same apply at the retail end and to fair trade organizations themselves?

Farmers' markets, alternative trading and public service networks, the internet – the potential of these and many more retail outlets has yet to be fully explored. What's more, people who are actively engaged by issues like human rights, peace or the environment are much more likely to buy fair trade. The movement must make its own contribution to this wider movement. So, for example, if a 'Tobin Tax' on currency speculation has a movement to go with it, why should not the fair trade movement promote a 'Fair Trade Tax' on commodity speculation?

The edifice of foul trade rests on the notion that price is not merely the best, but the only, arbiter of reason. In a competitive free market you get what you pay for. Everything else is suspect – too vulnerable to 'distortion' or 'political interference' to be relied upon.

However, the global market for commodities clearly does not behave competitively, while cheap commodities result from the political mechanisms of debt. Besides, as huge corporations consume each other and merge into an undifferentiated mass, the myth of fierce international competition is increasingly threadbare. Any competition tends to be between governments for the favor of corporations, or between impoverished people for a job, rather than between transnational conglomerates for a larger share of world markets they already control.

There is a long way still to go before fair trade makes any demonstrable impact on power structures such as these. Get impatient or deluded, give away the 'Fairtrade' label to Tesco and Starbucks, or hand over control to financial markets, and who is to say what they will not do with it?

What is fair?

Who is to decide, come to that, what is fair? That, too, is a political question. In recent decades, politically weakened peoples have been subjected to unrestrained free trade by vested interests which, at the same time, profit unashamedly from protectionism – its theoretical antithesis. Witness the infamous trading policies of the European Union or the corporate welfare provided by governments in the US, Japan and the North in general. In just one year, 2002, President George W Bush in his Farm Bill pledged an additional $180 billion of federal support for US industrial agriculture, and raised tariffs to protect US steel corporations. When the 'principles' of foul trade come up against its practice there is only ever one winner.

Political debate

Though the free trade thesis and protectionist antithesis are equally false, one might get closer to justice – and common sense – by turning them around. Genuinely democratic governments would surely represent the interests of their citizens, while setting corporate interests adrift in a world as free of government support and subsidy as they claim to wish it were. What that might mean for democracy or the state, the public or the private, regulation or deregulation, social movements or political programs remains, precisely, open to political debate.

There are some who argue that if free trade were to practice its principles and abandon protectionism in the North, then the South would be a clear and immediate winner.[9] There are others, like myself, who doubt whether free trade has any principles at all. The current Doha 'round' of trade negotiations – run by a World Trade Organization that has yet to defy a single significant corporate interest – offers few obvious reasons to conclude otherwise.

Either way, the allure of the mainstream is illusory. Small tributaries do not change its course; they are engulfed by it. And while the struggle for trade justice will continue with or without the 'Fairtrade' label, the reverse is much harder to envisage. For the time being at least the fair trade movement remains very much more than a niche filled with free-market nostrums. Short cuts tend to produce short circuits – and trust, once lost, can never be regained.

1 The Guardian, 2 February 2004. **2** Tesco press release, 1 March 2004. **3** The Sunday Times, 29 June 2003. **4** Press release, 5 September 2000, www.trans-fairusa.org **5** 'Coffee for two' by Alison Maitland, reprinted from The Financial Times in Developments, issue 28, 2004. **6** USA Today, 20 January 2004. **7** See for example, CaféDirect response, 5 May 2004, www.cafedirect.co.uk **8** 'What is to be done?', www.nestle.com **9** For example, Oxfam's report on trade, Rigged Rules and Double Standards. www.oxfam.org

Contacts and resources

Labeling

Many fairly traded products are now in the shops – if they are not, keep asking why not. Despite the debate about corporate involvement, an effective system of labeling is still needed to inform consumers, fend off fakers and encourage the rest.

The Fairtrade Labeling Organizations International (FLO) based in Bonn, Germany, is the umbrella body for all the major Fairtrade labels worldwide and can show you the ones to look out for wherever you live. **www.fairtrade.net**

Trading

There's an enormous range of fair trade products available through alternative outlets, which are always worth a visit. Here the label matters less than the organization – whether it's an aid agency or an alternative trading organization (ATO).

The International Fair Trade Association (IFAT) based in The Netherlands, is a global network of 160 organizations, many of them producers, in more than 50 countries. They are now entitled to use the Fair Trade Organization (FTO) mark, though it is not a product label. **www.ifat.org**

Campaigns

Perhaps even more encouraging than the spread of fair trade has been the growth of lively, well-informed and active engagement on trade issues worldwide. It would be impossible to list all the organizations doing wonderful work. Those listed here are recommended just as good places to start.

EUROPE

The Trade Justice Movement (TJM) in Britain is a fast-growing group of organizations including trade unions, aid agencies, environment and human rights campaigns, fair trade organizations, faith and consumer groups. Between them they have over nine million members. They are campaigning for trade justice – not free trade – with the rules weighted to benefit poor people and the environment. **www.tjm.org.uk**

NORTH AMERICA

Global Trade Watch (GTW) is a division of Public Citizen, the US national consumer and environmental group. GTW promotes government and corporate accountability in the globalization and trade arena. **www.citizen.org/trade**

AUSTRALASIA

AFTINET is an Australian network of over 90 community organizations and many more individuals concerned about trade and investment policy. It grew out of the successful campaign by community organizations against the Multilateral Agreement on Investment (MAI). **www.aftinet.org.au**

Contacts

WORLD
Focus on the Global South has offices in Bangkok, Mumbai and Manila. It aims to create a link between development at the grassroots and the 'macro' levels. Among other things, it mounts campaigns against trade liberalization promoted by neoliberal institutions and governments. **www.focusweb.org**

Third World Network is an independent non-profit international network of organizations and individuals involved in issues relating to development and North-South issues. Its international secretariat is based in Penang. It has offices in Delhi, Montevideo, Geneva and Accra. **www.twnside.org.sg**

BOOKS
There is a shortage of good books on this subject. **Fair Trade** by Michael Barratt Brown (Zed Books 1993) is a little outdated now, but it is still by far the best, coming as it did from a pivotal figure not just in thinking through the original ideas but in putting them into practice. More recently, **Fair Trade: Market-Driven Ethical Consumption** by Alex Nicholls and Charlotte Opal (Sage 2005) announces its approach, and its limitations, up-front in the title. But it does contain a lot of useful information.

The editions of the **New Internationalist** used in the text are as follows:
Coffee, No 271, September 1995
The Big Jeans Stitch-up, No 302, June 1998
The Cocoa Chain, No 304, August 1998
The Big Banana Split, No 317, October 1999
Fair Trade, No 322, April 2000
The World Trade Organization, No 334, May 2001
The Free Trade Game, No 374, December 2004
Trade Justice, No 388, May 2006
All can be found on the **NI** website at: **www.newint.org**

Index

Index

Index

302 659

NORTHERN COLLEGE LIBRARY
BARNSLEY S75 3ET